What Is the Future of Nanotechnology?

John Allen

ReferencePoint Press®

San Diego, CA

© 2017 ReferencePoint Press, Inc.
Printed in the United States

For more information, contact:
ReferencePoint Press, Inc.
PO Box 27779
San Diego, CA 92198
www. ReferencePointPress.com

LIBRARY OF CONGRESS CATALOGING-IN-PUBLICATION DATA

Names: Allen, John, 1957- author.
Title: What is the future of nanotechnology? / by John Allen.
Description: San Diego, CA : ReferencePoint Press, Inc., 2017. | 2016 |
Series: The future of technology | Audience: Grades 9-12. | Includes
bibliographical references and index.
Identifiers: LCCN 2015040503 (print) | LCCN 2015041698 (ebook) | ISBN
9781601529626 (hardback) | ISBN 9781601529633 (epub)
Subjects: LCSH: Nanotechnology--Juvenile literature. | Technological
innovations--Juvenile literature.
Classification: LCC T174.7 .A494 2017 (print) | LCC T174.7 (ebook) | DDC
620.5--dc23
LC record available at http://lccn.loc.gov/2015040503

Contents

Important Events in the Development of Nanotechnology

1959
American physicist Richard Feynman delivers a talk describing molecular machines building things atom by atom from the bottom up.

1983
Bell Laboratories researcher Louis E. Brus discovers semiconductor nanocrystals, more commonly known as *quantum dots.*

1974
Japanese scientist Norio Taniguchi uses the term *nanotechnology* in a conference on semiconductors.

1950	1960	1970	1980	1990

1981
American engineer K. Eric Drexler publishes a paper entitled "Molecular Engineering," which expands on Feynman's ideas.

1985
Two American scientists and a British astronomer discover spherical carbon molecules they name *buckyballs*.

1986
Drexler publishes the book *Engines of Creation: The Coming Era of Nanotechnology.*

1989
Scientists at IBM succeed in manipulating atoms to spell out the IBM corporate logo.

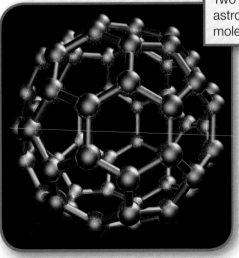

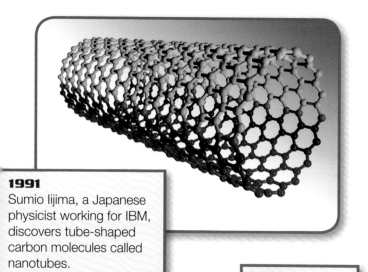

2013
Drexler publishes *Radical Abundance: How a Revolution in Nanotechnology Will Change Civilization.*

1991
Sumio Iijima, a Japanese physicist working for IBM, discovers tube-shaped carbon molecules called nanotubes.

1997
Zyvex, the first nanotechnology development company, is founded by software entrepreneur Jim Von Ehr.

2008
Ben Wang, an industrial engineering professor at Florida State University, invents *buckypaper* for use in fuel cells.

2014
Researchers at the University of Maryland create folded boxes made of graphene for hydrogen storage.

1995 **2000** **2005** **2010** **2015**

1993
The first Feynman Prize in Nanotechnology is awarded.

2005
Scientists at Cornell University create hybrid molecules shaped like buckyballs for targeted drug delivery.

2015
Researchers at IBM manufacture tiny 3D transistors using a molecular-scale technique called directed self-assembly.

2000
President Bill Clinton announces the National Nanotechnology Initiative.

2009
Scientists at Oxford University create a nanobot that can walk along a single strand of DNA.

Introduction

A Miniaturized Surgeon

From Theory to Application

Nanotechnology is a branch of engineering that involves the design and manufacture of things on the scale of molecules. Its products are measured by the nanometer, which is one-billionth of a meter, or about the width of four atoms. Nanotechnology—the prefix *nano* derives from the Greek word for dwarf—enables items to be built from the bottom up, atom by atom, with extreme precision. It will be used to create microscopic machines, from motors and robot arms to entire computers and factories. With its promise of manufacturing quality products at high speed and low cost, nanotechnology could one day bring the most fundamental changes to human society. It promises to have a huge impact on medicine, energy, warfare, and the environment. Scientists see it as an exponential technology, able to reproduce complex items as easily as a computer can copy data files.

In the 1966 film *Fantastic Voyage*, a crew aboard a miniaturized submarine travel through a famous scientist's bloodstream to seek and destroy a life-threatening blood clot. Fifty years later, science fiction is becoming fact. Scientists at the Swiss Federal Institute of Technology have developed tiny machines, called nanobots, to perform delicate medical procedures. According to Brad Nelson, an engineer and team leader at the Institute, "We're making microscopic robots that are guided by externally generated magnetic fields for use in the human body."[1] The nanobots can move through a patient's bloodstream to deliver medicine at a precise location. The ability of these tiny machines to reach difficult areas of the brain, heart, intestine, or urinary tract makes them an ideal tool to treat cancer, heart disease, and many other illnesses. And while surgeons would not be aboard a microscopic submarine as in the old movie, they would still be able to navigate inside the patient's body. In fact, nanosurgery would be something like a video game. "They would need training to learn how to use [the nanobots]," says Nelson, "but it's kind of an intuitive interface, and the nanobots would be guided with a joystick."[2]

A Technology Based on Nature

The idea of creating tiny machines that can be steered inside a person's bloodstream is part of nanotechnology, the science of things on a molecular scale. The American physicist Richard Feynman was the first to muse on the possibilities for such a technology, in 1959. Feynman saw no reason that modern physics could not create the ultimate manufacturing process: building objects by maneuvering atoms into place one by one. His ideas inspired the theorist K. Eric Drexler to imagine a revolution on the nanoscale to rival the digital revolution. "Imagine a world where the gadgets and goods that run our society are produced not in a far-flung supply chain of industrial facilities, but in compact, even desktop-scale, machines," says Drexler. "Then imagine that the technologies that can make these visions real are emerging—under many names, behind the scenes, with a long road still ahead, yet moving surprisingly fast."[3]

> **WORDS IN CONTEXT**
>
> **nanoscale**
> Measured in nanometers, each of which is one-billionth of a meter.

Drexler believes that nanotechnology will one day enable scientists and engineers to fabricate virtually anything, from minerals, crops, and fuels to large, complex machines. Such a breakthrough, Drexler insists, could produce abundant food and water, clothing, shelter, and other necessities of life. Poverty would disappear. People would live longer, healthier, and richer lives. The

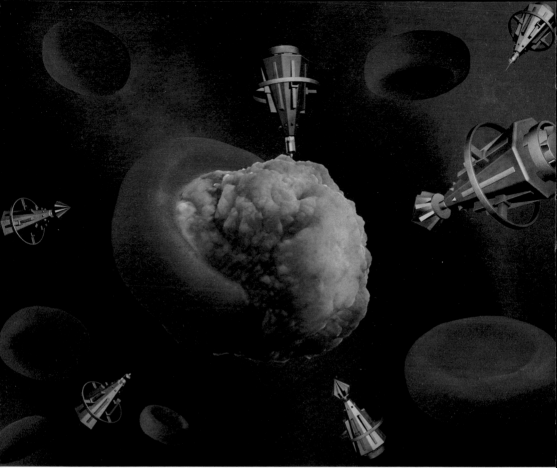

Nanobots (depicted in an illustration) attack a germ in the bloodstream. In 1959 US physicist Richard Feynman mused on the possibility of tiny machines that could be built atom by atom.

human imagination would have at its disposal the greatest creative tool of all.

Such claims for nanotechnology may sound exaggerated. However, its supporters say there is plenty of proof that atomically precise engineering is feasible. Its products are everywhere as part of nature. It is atomic structure that makes a heart different from a pancreas, iron ore different from diamonds. As scientists in the twentieth century unlocked the secrets of atoms and molecules, they also learned how to manipulate these building blocks of matter. Chemists linked molecules in complex chains to form plastics and synthetic fibers. Biologists found they could alter human genes in the DNA molecule to treat or prevent disease. These accomplishments mimic, in a simpler way, what nature has been doing on an atomic level for billions of years. Nanotechnology promises to use the laws of physics and chemistry to harness the abundance of nature.

The Promise of Tiny Breakthroughs

Predictions for the future of nanotechnology have mostly gone unfulfilled so far. Molecular manufacturing remains a theoretical prospect. As with other cutting-edge technologies, such as gene therapy, early enthusiasm has been dampened somewhat due to slower progress than expected. Yet companies worldwide continue to spend billions on research in the field. Many industries already employ versions of nanotechnology to improve everyday products, such as fabrics, floor coverings, and building materials. Computers rely on microcircuits scarcely larger than a blood cell. Medical uses, such as targeted drug delivery, may soon lead to tiny sensors in the body, able to alert doctors to the presence of viruses or cancer cells. Nanotechnology promises to bring huge changes to almost every facet of life, including medicine, energy and the environment, and warfare.

Along with these breakthroughs will come serious concerns. A technology based on particles too small to see raises the question of terrorist threats, such as toxic molecules or nanobots capable of sabotage. Tiny sensors could be used for surveillance of citizens by rogue governments. Molecular manufacturing could disrupt the world's economy in unforeseen ways. Nanotechnology, with its ability to manipulate matter at the atomic level, will present many new challenges for the future.

> **WORDS IN CONTEXT**
>
> **nanotechnology**
> The branch of technology that deals with engineering things at the molecular scale.

Chapter 1

The History of Nanotechnology

On December 29, 1959, the American physicist Richard Feynman addressed the annual West Coast meeting of the American Physical Society at the California Institute of Technology. Before the gathered scientists, Feynman introduced a novel topic:

> What I want to talk about is the problem of manipulating and controlling things on a small scale. As soon as I mention this, people tell me about miniaturization, and how far it has progressed today. . . . There is a device on the market, they tell me, by which you can write the Lord's Prayer on the head of a pin. But that's nothing; that's the most primitive, halting step in the direction I intend to discuss. . . . *Why cannot we write the entire 24 volumes of the Encyclopedia Britannica on the head of a pin?*[4]

Feynman went on to discuss the practical aspects of such a feat. It would be necessary, he pointed out, to reduce the text in the encyclopedia by twenty-five thousand times. Each dot in the book's half-tone photos would measure about thirty-two atoms across. He calculated that if all the books in the libraries of the world could be reduced the same way, they would fill about thirty-five pages of the encyclopedia. To emphasize the enormous amount of storage possible in an amazingly small space, Feynman called his talk "There's Plenty of Room at the Bottom."[5] However, true to his visionary nature (and probably in hopes of dazzling his colleagues), Feynman took his idea much further. Many consider this talk the beginning of nanotechnology.

Building Things Atom by Atom

Feynman imagined a process of manufacturing things on a very small scale, not just microscopic, but submicroscopic. His idea for how to scale down the machinery was ingenious. He proposed building a mechanism that could manufacture parts and tools that are one-quarter the size of the master tools. The smaller mechanism would then perform the same steps, also at one-quarter size, resulting in a system one-sixteenth the size of the original mechanism. Feynman declared that this process could continue until the manufacturing machinery reached the nanoscale. He even suggested that the whole process could be controlled, through electronics, by the original, normal-size equipment. Feynman's method called for the assembly of complex devices, including miniscule computers, too small to be seen with the naked eye—this at a time when actual computers were so large they filled entire rooms. He proposed building a billion tiny factories, all exactly alike, and each capable of molding parts, drilling holes, and assembling items just like full-size factories. To encourage research into such miniaturization, Feynman raised what he considered two formidable challenges. He offered a prize of $1,000 to the first person who could place the information on the page of an ordinary book in an area 1/25,000 smaller in scale, and another $1,000 to anyone who could make an operating electric motor tiny enough to fit inside a 1/64-inch cube.

Feynman pursued his idea to its logical extreme. "But I am not afraid to consider the final question," he announced, "as to whether, ultimately—in the great future—we can arrange the atoms the way we want; the very *atoms,* all the way down!"[6] Feynman imagined that such a capability could produce substances with an incredible range of properties unknown in nature. Products could be made from the bottom up, perfectly identical and flawless, by arranging their atoms with great precision. He declared that no laws of physics prevented such an undertaking and that in fact the most intricate processes in biology occur on the atomic level.

Nanotechnology takes place at the submicroscopic level, meaning a world so small it cannot be seen even with a light microscope. The unit of measurement in nanotechnology, the nanometer, is one-billionth of a meter. This is much, much smaller than a centimeter, a millimeter, or a micrometer. In fact, a nanometer is a hundred-thousandth the width of a single human hair. A comparison between the head of a pin, a single particle of ragweed pollen, a red blood cell, and a carbon nanotube (a tube-shaped carbon molecule that is much stronger than steel) illustrates the scale of nanotechnology.

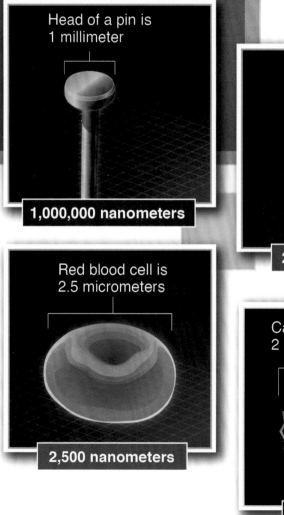

Head of a pin is 1 millimeter

1,000,000 nanometers

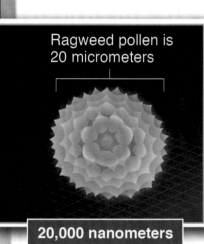

Ragweed pollen is 20 micrometers

20,000 nanometers

Red blood cell is 2.5 micrometers

2,500 nanometers

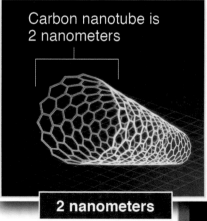

Carbon nanotube is 2 nanometers

2 nanometers

Feynman liked his talk so much that he published it the following year in the Caltech house magazine, *Engineering and Science*. Scientists disagree on how influential Feynman's lecture was among their colleagues. For the next twenty years there were few citations to it in scientific journals, a fact that Feynman himself acknowledged in a follow-up talk in 1983. "Feynman had a dream, but he did not come up with a blueprint," says Fraser Stoddart, who has done pioneering work on nanotechnology at Northwestern University in Evanston, Illinois. "Yet it would have been asking a lot of him to see much beyond what he did see and predict."[7] Mark Ratner, a chemist at Northwestern University, sees Feynman as a great inspiration to scientists in the new field. "Bold speculative visions are wonderful, and imagination is crucial to the development and introduction of new scientific ideas," says Ratner. "And imagination was Feynman's great stock in trade."[8]

Popularizing Nanotechnology

Feynman's vision received wider attention thanks to American engineer K. Eric Drexler. In 1981 Drexler published a paper entitled "Molecular Engineering," which mentioned Feynman in the first sentence. Drexler expanded on the idea of creating machines that work on the molecular level to build things atom by atom from the bottom up. His 1986 book *Engines of Creation: The Coming Era of Nanotechnology* introduced general readers to the word *nanotechnology* and the underlying concept of manipulating matter on the nanoscale. (Unbeknownst to Drexler, Norio Taniguchi, a Japanese scientist in Tokyo, had first used the term *nanotechnology* at a 1974 conference on semiconductors.) Drexler developed his own powerful ideas about the paths nanotechnology might take. He described armies of nanoscale robots that could patrol a patient's bloodstream in search of viral invaders or arterial blockages. Seizing on Feynman's notion of a billion tiny factories, Drexler imagined billions of nanobots armed with the capability to reproduce themselves endlessly. He called the uncontrollable spread of these virus-like machines "grey goo" and warned that they could cover the world. "Grey goo is what would happen if one of the auto-assemblers went haywire and the self-replication never stopped," writes *New York Times* reporter Lawrence Osborne. "According to Drexler's calculations, in just 10 hours an unchecked self-replicating auto-assembler would spawn 68 billion offspring; in less than two days the auto-assemblers would outweigh the earth."[9]

Scientists insisted that Drexler's doomsday scenario, should it even be possible, lay far in the future. Drexler now regrets using the term "grey goo," which gave readers the impression that nanotechnology represents science gone out of control. He remains, however, a strong advocate for nanotechnology through his books and speeches. An updated account of his ideas is found in the 2013 book *Radical Abundance: How a Revolution in Nanotechnology Will Change Civilization.* In it Drexler focuses on atomically precise manufacturing (APM), which is based on Feynman's vision of making things by manipulating atoms into place. For many scientists and futurists, APM is the ultimate goal of nanotechnology—a sort of replicator as imagined in science fiction shows like *Star Trek*—providing humankind with the ability to satisfy its material needs and desires in astonishing ways. Drexler compares the coming APM era to the rapid spread of digital technology. "APM holds the potential," he writes, "for a physical revolution that, if unconstrained, could unfold at the speed of the new digital media."[10]

Breakthroughs on the Nanoscale

The basis for such a revolution was established by important breakthroughs in the 1980s. Perhaps the most crucial advance was the ability to obtain more detailed images of actual atoms. In 1981 two IBM researchers, Gerd Binnig and Heinrich Rohrer, invented the scanning tunneling microscope (STM). This device, the most powerful microscope yet conceived, is considered the gateway to nanotechnology. The electron microscope, which had improved upon optical devices that employed lenses, was unable to view individual atoms clearly. To create a better microscope,

The scanning tunneling microscope, or STM, (pictured) is considered the gateway to nanotechnology. The STM enables researchers to see detailed images of atoms—and even move them around with great precision.

Binnig and Rohrer began to experiment with tunneling. This is a phenomenon from quantum mechanics in which atoms break away from the surface of a substance and form a cloud hovering just above it. When another solid surface approaches with its own cloud of electrons, the two electron clouds can overlap, causing

Tackling Feynman's Nanotechnology Challenges

In his famous 1959 lecture raising the possibility of nanotechnology, physicist Richard Feynman issued two challenges to scientists and engineers to see if the problems of radical miniaturization could be solved in a practical way. Each challenge carried with it a prize of $1,000 for success—no small sum in 1959.

Feynman's second challenge was the first to be met and proved to be rather simple. Feynman offered his prize to the first person who could make an operating electric motor that was controlled from the outside and could fit inside a 1/64-inch cube. It took William McLellan, an engineer at Caltech, only a few months working on his lunch breaks to claim the prize. McLellan's handmade device—he actually made ten of them for good measure—had thirteen parts, weighed 250 micrograms, and was fashioned with the use of tweezers, toothpicks, and paintbrushes. "[Feynman] really didn't believe it could be done," says McLellan. "But he found out."

The first challenge, which involved shrinking the information on a book page into an area 1/25,000 smaller in scale, proved more difficult. In 1985, twenty-six years after Feynman's talk, a Stanford University graduate student named Tom Newman wrote to Feynman asking if the book-page prize had ever been claimed. Feynman phoned to encourage Newman to pursue it. Working with a colleague, Newman miniaturized the first page of Charles Dickens's *A Tale of Two Cities* using electron-beam lithography. Feynman's task, which once seemed impossible, proved to be no match for modern technology.

Quoted in Royal Society of Chemistry, "Feynman's Fancy," January 2009. www.rsc.org.

a flow of electric current. Binnig and Rohrer found that moving a sharp metal tip closely over the surface of a metal sample produced an electrical current between tip and surface that could be measured with great precision. Variations in the current provided data about the sample's surface and inner structure that could be used to make a three-dimensional map of the metal on the atomic scale. Their first experiment with a crystal of gold produced amazing images of precisely spaced atoms that seemed to form steps and terraces. "I couldn't stop looking at the images," Binnig recalls. "It was entering a new world."[11]

Binnig and Rohrer went on to improve the mechanical design of the device, producing images of even greater clarity. As the STM reached scientists around the world, it was hailed as an amazing new tool for studying matter on the atomic scale. The STM also enabled them to move individual atoms around with great precision, a capability once thought impossible. It opened the field of nanotechnology to many new researchers. In 1986 Binnig and Rohrer's invention earned them the Nobel Prize in Physics. That same year Binnig developed the atomic force microscope, which could provide even more precise atomic-scale images of materials. Other inventors built on the work of Binnig and Rohrer to produce refined devices and techniques for viewing and manipulating atoms. In 1989 scientists at IBM succeeded in making a playful demonstration of the new technology. They used an STM to nudge thirty-five atoms of the element xenon precisely into place on a nickel surface, spelling out the IBM corporate logo.

Buckyballs and Nanotubes

The next milestone in nanotechnology began with one of nature's most common atoms: carbon. Atoms of carbon can form diamond, nature's hardest known material, and graphite, which is one of the softest. Carbon atoms are found in DNA, and they bond easily with many other elements. In 1985 the British astronomer Harold Kroto joined American scientists Richard Smalley and Robert Curl to study a puzzling phenomenon. Kroto wondered about the long chains of carbon atoms that his instruments detected from Red Giant stars billions of miles away. He asked himself how such chains or clusters could come together. Smalley and Curl had investigated similar chains of carbon atoms in the laboratory. The three scientists managed to simulate the massive heat and pressure of a Red Giant by putting graphite in a helium-filled chamber and vaporizing it with a powerful laser. The experiment produced carbon molecules that each contained exactly 60 carbon atoms arranged in the shape of a hollow sphere, much like the pattern of seams on a soccer ball. It was the most symmetrical large molecule yet discovered. Kroto was reminded of a futuristic shape from architecture—the geodesic dome popularized by American architect Buckminster Fuller in the 1930s. Thereafter the unusual spherical molecules of carbon were called fullerenes or buckyballs, after Fuller. A single molecule was called C60, for its chemical shorthand name.

Buckyballs, like a fancy new toy, created a sensation in the scientific world. The molecules proved to possess a number of unusual properties. Scientists found they could bounce, spin at incredible speeds, and return to their original shape after being squeezed or rammed. Further research showed buckyballs to be shock resistant and also possessing qualities of superconductivity. In 1990 scientists in the United States and Germany sent an arc of electricity between two sticks of carbon, creating a vapor that condensed to a sooty gob teeming with buckyballs. Using a variation of this process, Sumio Iijima, a Japanese physicist working for IBM, produced tube-shaped carbon molecules, called nanotubes.

Nanotubes represent the fourth elemental form of carbon, after diamond, graphite, and buckyballs. They may yet prove to be the most important. According to *Businessweek* magazine, carbon nanotubes are "a material invisible to the naked eye yet harder than diamonds and many times stronger than steel."[12] The first nanotubes were actually tubes within tubes, with a somewhat messy inner structure. However, chemists discovered how to make more elegant versions consisting of a single layer of carbon atoms—with the buckyball "soccer ball" arrangement—and a hollow space inside. Each nanotube can be up to a millimeter in length and consist of more than one million atoms.

These high-quality nanotubes hold vast potential for creating light but very strong industrial materials, microscopic computer

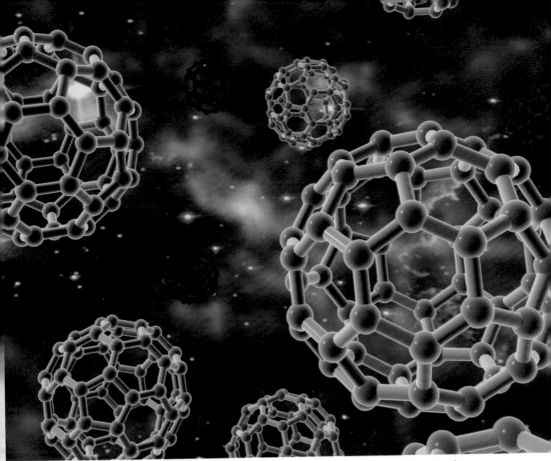

The spherical carbon molecules called buckyballs (pictured) have several unusual properties. They can bounce, spin rapidly, and return to their original shape after being squeezed or rammed; they also have qualities of superconductivity.

chips, tiny batteries for automobiles and electronics, and ultraefficient power lines. They are used today to make everything from lightweight tennis racquets to special clothing that protects from the sun's ultraviolet radiation. Their hollow structure enables them to act as tiny filters, with small molecules passing through but larger objects such as bacteria and viruses held out. Nanotubes also are attached to the tips of atomic force microscope probes, making them sharper and more sensitive. This not only allows for higher resolution images—down to single atoms—but also makes the probe more durable and improves its ability to push and pull atoms into place. In short, much of the nanotechnology research performed worldwide is made possible by the combination of the atomic force microscope and the carbon nanotube, a state of affairs that seems likely to continue.

Government Support and Private Investment

Breakthroughs like the discovery of the nanotube in 1991 brought new interest from governments and private investors. Suddenly nanotechnology became one of the hottest topics in science. That same year the Japanese Ministry of International Trade and Industry (MITI) launched an ambitious ten-year Atom Technology project. Financed with a government grant of more than $200 million and including thirty-nine Japanese technology firms and seven foreign companies, the project aimed to study how to control the movement of atoms and molecules with precision. Experts described the project as a sort of atom factory, dedicated to bottom-up manufacturing on the atomic scale akin to the ideas of Feynman and Drexler. The first Feynman Prize in Nanotechnology, focused on scientists who advance Feynman's vision of molecular manufacturing, was awarded in 1993. In 1996 nanotechnology made worldwide news with the announcement that Kroto, Smalley, and Curl had won the Nobel Prize for Chemistry for their discovery of buckyballs, those intriguing clusters of carbon atoms.

The perceived importance of a new technology is often judged by the amount of funding it attracts. In 2000 nanotechnology research in the United States received a huge boost with President Bill Clinton's announcement of the National Nanotechnology Initiative (NNI). The initiative sought to link nanotechnology-related scientists and research efforts inside the United States and around the world. Federal funding for the NNI quickly expanded to $495 million, and that total was exceeded by further investments from states, universities, and corporations. The NNI enlisted several government agencies, including the Department of Defense, the Department of Energy, NASA, and the National Institutes of Health, in the quest for new nanoscale applications. By 2015 funding for the NNI had grown to more than $1.5 billion. Private investment in nanotechnology dwarfed the federal effort. In 2008 the Food and Drug Law Institute estimated that more than $60 billion in manufactured goods worldwide incorporated some form of nano-

The Foresight Institute

In 1986 *Engines of Creation* author K. Eric Drexler and his then-wife Christine Peterson founded the Foresight Institute in Palo Alto, California. The institute's original goal was to promote the couple's vision for the emerging field of nanotechnology, focusing on atomically precise manufacturing, the idea that products can be built atom by atom from the bottom up. From the beginning Peterson and Drexler sought to educate policy makers and the public about physicist Richard Feynman's vision of building factories that operate on the atomic level. In the 1990s they introduced the Feynman Prizes in Nanotechnology. These are two prizes of $10,000 that are awarded annually to important work in the categories of Theoretical and Experimental Nanotechnology. The Foresight Institute also offers a $250,000 Feynman Grand Prize. This award is reserved for the creation of one of two breakthroughs: a nanoscale robotic arm capable of positional control with great precision; and a nanoscale 8-bit adder, or digital circuit, for adding numbers. No scientists or engineers have yet been able to claim this prize.

The institute's annual awards show the amazing variety of work being done in the field. The 2014 Theory award went to Australian scientist Dr. Amanda S. Barnard for her unique method of computing the stability of diamond nanostructures. Dr. Joseph W. Lyding, a professor at the University of Illinois, received the 2014 Experimental award for his work using a scanning tunneling microscope to transfer patterns and structures onto surfaces at the atomic scale.

technology. Some experts predict that the global market for nanotechnology will soon top $1 trillion.

Other market analysts insist these numbers are far too high. According to Michael Berger, founder of Nanowerk LLC, "These trillion-dollar forecasts for an artificially constructed 'market' are an irritating, sensationalist and unfortunate way of saying that sooner or later nanotechnologies will have a deeply transformative impact on more or less all aspects of our lives."[13] As with other cutting-edge technologies, such as genetic engineering, the feverish speculation and exaggerated predictions about nanotechnology have outpaced the reality. For example, despite the amazing qualities of buckyballs and their seemingly endless potential, scientists have struggled to find practical uses for them. Nonetheless, many everyday products, from automobiles with scratch-resistant paint to tennis balls with durable coating, do feature aspects of nano-technology, with thousands more on the way. One celebrated na-noscale breakthrough from the 1980s is now on the verge of being a household fixture. In 1983 Louis E. Brus, a researcher at AT&T Bell Laboratories, discovered semiconductor nanocrystals, more commonly called quantum dots—clusters of hundreds and thou-sands of atoms whose electrons exhibit energy levels as if they made up a single atom. Today quantum dots, which erupt into various colors when exposed to UV light, are being incorporat-ed into the latest flat-screen televisions. Researchers predict that quantum dots will provide enhanced image quality to televisions at a lower cost—one more way in which nanotechnology promises to improve people's daily lives.

Chapter 2

Surgeons in the Bloodstream

Patients generally hope that their surgical procedure will be over quickly. Harvard physicist Eric Mazur can offer the ultimate reassurance: The procedure will only take a billionth of a second. That is how long it takes Mazur's femtosecond laser to vaporize a single mitochondrion within a living cell. (A mitochondrion is the part of a cell that serves as its power plant, breaking down glucose and transferring energy.) In this technique of laser nanosurgery, the operating room fits under a powerful microscope—or actually a system of microscopes. The devices work together to focus the laser with such concentrated energy that it rivals the heat of the sun. "We start by squeezing a huge amount of light into a very small space," says Mazur. "It's done in much the same way that you might use a magnifying glass to focus rays of sunshine."[14] The awesome power of the beam reaches only the target, leaving the rest of the cell unharmed. This is possible due to the laser's operating speed. Each pulse of the beam lasts one hundred femtoseconds, which is a millionth of a billionth of a second. Mazur's special laser presents exciting possibilities for the future of nanosurgery. "One of the most exciting results is how this new laser scalpel moves surgery down in scale," he says, "from using a traditional scalpel to perform surgery on an organism to performing it at the cellular level. At this scale, we can micro-manipulate the machinery of life."[15]

> **WORDS IN CONTEXT**
>
> **femtosecond**
> A unit of time equal to one-quadrillionth of a second.

Nanoparticles That Act like Good Cholesterol

Two kinds of particles move the fatty, waxy substance known as cholesterol through the bloodstream. One kind is labeled "bad" because it deposits cholesterol on the walls of blood vessels, causing potential blockages. The other kind is "good" because it sweeps the cholesterol on to the liver to be excreted. Scientists are developing nanoparticles that mimic the good transporters by gathering up cholesterol before it can accumulate into deadly plaque deposits. The new particles have surfaces coated with fats and proteins to collect the sticky cholesterol from arterial walls and whisk it through the bloodstream. Preventing cholesterol from forming deposits is key to heading off strokes and heart attacks.

Dr. Andre Nel, who leads the study at the Center for Environmental Implications of Nanotechnology at the University of California in Los Angeles, says the nanoparticles could someday become an important tool for treating cardiovascular disease. Another promising technique is to equip nanoparticles with tiny bits of RNA, the chemical cousin of DNA. Researchers at MIT have found that RNA can be engineered to interfere with the metabolism of cholesterol, cutting its harmful version by as much as two-thirds. Nanoparticles could also be used for monitoring blood cholesterol for early signs of danger. Nanoparticles filled with gold or iron oxide can be tracked with medical imaging devices to reveal plaque building up on arterial walls.

The Cutting Edge of Medicine

Mazur's technique for operating on organelles, which are specialized parts inside living cells, is merely one possible approach in the field of nanosurgery. With today's focus on surgical techniques that are less invasive, nanosurgery, with its ability to target tiny areas and even individual cells with great delicacy, would seem to have endless potential. Most biological materials are transparent, so lasers like the one used by Mazur, which operates on visible light, can pass through them at great speed without causing damage. Such capabilities have led many experts to predict a coming revolution in surgery on the nanoscale, with an array of products and techniques currently in development. "Nanosurgery research may still be in its infancy," says Marie Freebody, a science writer and editor, "but with so many exciting breakthroughs in the field, there can be little doubt that this mighty tool is coming to a surgery table near you."[16]

Laser nanosurgery is the result of decades of research on the subatomic world. The invention of the electron microscope in 1931 provided scientists with their first glimpse of matter at the nanoscale. It was not until the 1950s that manipulation at this scale became possible, enabling researchers to surgically remove mitochondria from cells in the laboratory. Invention of the first lasers in the early 1960s provided a tool that has led to undreamt-of precision in probing and manipulating cells and cell parts.

Nanosurgery also allows scientists to study biological processes in new ways. Mehmet Fatih Yanik, a researcher at the Massachusetts Institute of Technology (MIT) in Cambridge, Massachusetts, and Adela Ben-Yakar, a mechanical engineer at the University of Texas in Austin, have used this ultrafast laser surgery technique to sever neurons in tiny living roundworms. The high-speed laser pulses allow the researchers to "operate" on the worms without having to immobilize them with anesthetics, which can interfere with the process of nerve regrowth. They then are able to study how the nerves regenerate and develop. Like Mazur, these researchers rely on nanosurgery for its amazing precision. According to Ben-Yakar, "It goes without saying that collateral damage is not an option when surrounding tissue may actually provide a structural cue to regeneration."[17] Yanik and Ben-Yakar hope to use their findings to develop drug and gene therapies to improve nerve regeneration. Their research could lead to major breakthroughs in treating nerve damage in humans. In addition Ben-Yakar and her group are using nanosurgery for cancer treatment, particularly breast cancer. One technique involves the use of gold nanoparticles, which actually were discovered by the English scientist Michael Faraday in the nineteenth century. These gold nanoparticles can be injected into a patient's system and then serve as microscopic magnifying lenses to focus

> **WORDS IN CONTEXT**
>
> **nanoparticle**
> A microscopic particle that behaves as a whole unit in terms of its movement and properties.

laser energy on targeted cells. The nanoparticles actually increase the laser light reaching cancer cells tenfold, producing bursts of intense heat. "If we can consistently deliver nanoparticles to cancer cells or other tissue that we want to target, we would be able to remove hundreds of unwanted cells at once using a single femtosecond laser pulse," Ben-Yakar says. "But we would still be keeping the healthy cells alive while photo-damaging just the cells we want, basically creating nanoscale holes in a tissue."[18] Ben-Yakar and other researchers hope that the laser microscalpel will one day be a commonplace tool for cancer surgery and other procedures.

During eye surgery, a femtosecond laser slices the cornea to create a cap that will be put back in place after additional procedures are performed. This type of laser can be used to manipulate the structures found inside of cells.

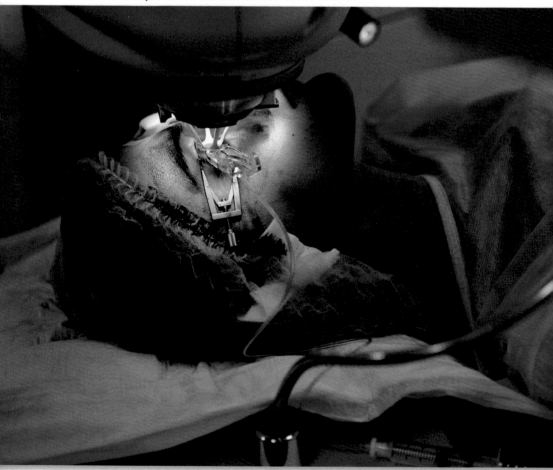

Promising Nanoparticles

Similar hopes surround the medical use of nanoparticles. Already there are nearly fifty biomedical products on the market that feature nanoparticles, and dozens more are moving rapidly through the research pipeline in late-stage clinical trials. According to the American Society for Testing and Materials, a nanoparticle is defined as ranging in size from one to one hundred nanometers. By contrast, a sheet of paper is about one hundred thousand nanometers thick and a human hair measures about seventy-five thousand nanometers in diameter. Nanoparticles can be made of gold, silver, carbon, cadmium, and other materials. In the beginning researchers focused on using them for targeted drug delivery, but their potential in many other areas is now being recognized.

In 2005 scientists at Cornell University in Ithaca, New York, were able to create hybrid molecules in the shape of buckyballs from DNA and polystyrene, a kind of plastic. The hybrid molecules spontaneously assembled themselves into hollow balls about four hundred nanometers in diameter. The researchers designed the buckyballs to carry drugs into cells, where natural enzymes would break down the DNA and release the drug. Like other experimenters, however, the Cornell group had trouble steering the hybrid buckyballs in a way that was not too costly and time-consuming. Eight years later engineers at Columbia University in New York City came up with their own buckyball design for drug delivery. They managed to isolate a single water molecule inside a buckyball. This allowed them to move the larger buckyball molecule by controlling the smaller water molecule with a special electric field. So far this seems one of the most promising methods of delivering drugs via nanoparticles.

Robert Langer, a professor of Chemical and Biomedical Engineering at MIT, is excited about the prospects for nanoparticles in fighting diseases like cancer, but he cautions that delivery is only part of the challenge. "Our laboratories are working on a number of problems related to medical nanotechnology," Langer says.

> One is, can we get a high-yield sort of drug encapsulated in the nanoparticles? Two—can we create nanoparticles that will be very specifically targeted to specific cell types,

like say, prostate cancer? Three—can we put more complex drugs . . . in them? Four—can we demonstrate that they work in animal models? And five—can we work with people, clinicians and companies, to show that they work in human models?"[19]

Langer thinks nanoparticles could eventually be used in gene therapy, to enter cells and shut genes off or turn them on in order to treat genetic diseases.

Nanoparticles for Fighting Cancer

Nanoparticles also could play a large role in fighting various kinds of cancer, for which early detection can make a lifesaving difference. The key to early diagnosis is detecting so-called biomarkers that show the presence of cancer in the body. Cancer results when abnormal cells begin to grow uncontrollably. To become cancer cells, normal cells go through a multistep process that permanently alters each cell and its descendants. These altered cells acquire traits that enable them to evade the body's defense mechanisms and continue to spread. For example, they gain the ability to divide on their own, resist signals to stop growing, and evade apoptosis, or the usual programmed death of cells. Yet cancer cells, like neighboring healthy cells, still add to the composition of proteins in the blood. Scientists theorize that these protein biomarkers could be used to detect cancer at a very early stage. The problem is that early tumor cells represent very low concentrations compared to healthy cells. Somehow the distracting "noise" of the vastly more numerous healthy cells has to be filtered out in order to detect the few cancerous biomarkers. And that is where nanoparticles come in.

Scientists at Brazil's University of Sao Paulo and Spain's Institute of Microelectronics of Madrid are teaming up to create a new kind of biosensor. They hope to use silicon and gold nanoparticles as tiny sensors to detect ultralow concentrations of cancer

A tray containing cancer cells will be used in research at a London nanomedicine lab. Researchers are experimenting with nanoparticles that may be able to detect the presence of cancer at a very early stage.

biomarkers. Their nanosensors are able to identify the very few precancerous cells among healthy ones, capture the cancerous markers using special antibodies, and tag them. The researchers have successfully detected extremely low concentrations of cancer biomarkers for colon and prostate cancer. They believe their technique could one day be used for early detection of cancer through routine blood tests.

Other researchers are using nanoparticles equipped with special probes for recognizing tumor cells that are shed into the bloodstream from growing tumors. Short strands of DNA or RNA can be added to gold nanoparticles to seek out and bind to targeted cells. These aptamers, as the probes are called, have shown success in finding and identifying different subtypes of leukemia, a blood cancer, in concentrations as low as ten cells per milliliter of blood. The aptamers on nanoparticles can also be programmed to find other specific cancers, including lung, liver, ovarian, breast, and brain. Nanoparticles with aptamers also show great promise for delivering anticancer drugs to diseased cells. "The prototype of targeted drug delivery can be traced back to the concept of a 'magic bullet,' proposed by chemotherapy pioneer and 1908 Nobel laureate Paul Ehrlich," writes Guizhi Zhu, a chemist at the Health Cancer Center at the University of Florida. "Ehrlich envisioned a drug that could selectively target a disease-causing organism or diseased cells, leaving healthy tissue unharmed. A century later, researchers are developing many types of nanoscale 'magic bullets' that can specifically deliver drugs into target cells or tissues."[20]

Yet another promising cancer treatment is the use of nanoparticles to bolster a patient's immune system. Researchers at Johns Hopkins University in Baltimore, Maryland, set out to rapidly multiply white blood cells, or T cells, due to their cancer-fighting potential. To do this, they created artificial magnetic nanoparticles that can interact with so-called naïve T cells—those arising from the immune system's production in the bone marrow—that are in the bloodstream. The custom-made nanoparticles bind to special receptors on the surfaces of the T cells and equip them with specific proteins called antigens. This programs the T cells to attack tumor cells and to make more T cells. The problem is overcoming the scarcity of naïve T cells in the blood. By running blood plasma through a magnetic column, the tumor-fighting T cells bound to the nanoparticles stick to the sides of the column, allowing unwanted cells to wash through. The result is a concentration of naïve T cells that can then be quickly expanded in a culture by five thousand or ten thousand times. Suddenly the patient has an immune system more capable of warding off cancer or serious infections. "The challenge has been to train these cells efficiently enough, and get them to divide fast enough, that we could use them as the basis of a therapy for cancer patients," says Jonathan Schneck, a professor at Johns Hopkins' Institute for Cell Engineering. "We've taken a big step toward solving that problem."[21]

Swallowing the Surgeon

Many problems related to diagnosing and treating diseases may someday be solved by nanobots—microscopic robots so small that billions of them fit in a teaspoon. The idea goes back to Richard Feynman's famous talk in 1959. "It would be interesting in surgery if you could swallow the surgeon," Feynman suggested. "You put the mechanical surgeon inside the blood vessel and it goes into the heart and 'looks' around. . . . It finds out which valve is the faulty one and takes a little knife and slices it out. Other small machines might be permanently incorporated in the body to assist some inadequately functioning organ."[22]

An Array of Medical Nanobots

Robert Freitas thinks the future of medicine belongs to nanobots, bacterium-size robots that can help the body repair itself. To this end he designs nanobots to accomplish specific tasks inside a patient's body. For example, one of his inventions could rescue a person who is choking or treat someone who suffers from ischemia, a restriction in blood supply that causes a shortage of oxygen to vital organs. His invention is mechanical red blood cells called respirocytes, made of nanoscale components. The spherical robotic cells, with their pressurized shells of pure diamond, could hold 236 times more oxygen and carbon dioxide than human red blood cells. They could provide oxygen to a person's bloodstream rapidly and efficiently. They would even enable a person to sprint at top speed for fifteen minutes. The only problem with respirocytes is that the technology to assemble them does not yet exist.

Freitas, a researcher at the Institute for Molecular Manufacturing, has no doubt that nanoscale factories capable of making an endless supply of nanobots will one day be a reality. "With diligent effort," he says, "the first fruits of this advanced nanomedicine could begin to appear in clinical treatment sometime during the 2020s." In the meantime he continues to design nanobots for the future. Perhaps his most radical design is the chromallocyte, a lozenge-shaped nanobot for replacing chromosomes inside cells. Chromallocytes could potentially remove defective, disease-causing chromosomes and replace them with healthy versions. Such a procedure could slow down—or even halt—the aging process.

Robert A. Freitas Jr., "The Future of Nanomedicine," *The Futurist*. www.wfs.org.

Feynman's vision of a tiny robot wielding a tiny knife inside a person's body may seem like something out of a futuristic cartoon. However, surgical nanobots are a serious innovation that may soon become a standard medical tool. One example is the OctoMag system developed by researchers at the Multi-Scale Robotics Lab in Zurich, Switzerland. The system operates a microrobot about four times the width of a human hair. It uses eight electromagnetic coils to push and pull the tiny robot wirelessly. The Zurich team has tested the microrobot for eye surgery by navigating it safely through the eye of a rabbit entirely by energy from magnetic fields.

The team's next challenge is to decrease the robot's size even further, to the nanoscale. Since magnetic force drops considerably at this scale, the scientists hope to propel the nanobots by giving them rotating appendages, like a bacterium's rotary motor, enabling them to rotate like corkscrews through viscous liquid. "More than three billion years ago, bacteria evolved a swimming strategy at micrometer dimensions that nature had difficulty improving upon," explains Simone Schürle, a researcher at the Zurich lab. "Our [artificial bacterial flagella] represents the first demonstration of wireless swimming microrobots similar in size and geometry to natural bacterial flagella, and are many orders of magnitude smaller. . . . The potential impact of this technology on society is high, particularly for biomedical applications."[23] Using 3D laser nanolithography, a sort of microscopic 3D printing process, the Zurich team is able to fabricate armies of thousands of swimming nanobots for surgery. A syringeful of the nanobots could be tracked through a patient's body to treat cancerous tumors or blood clots.

The Future for Surgical Nanobots

In the future surgical nanobots could perform a variety of tasks inside the patient, from delivering drugs to examining and repairing cells or tissues to eliminating unwanted cells. Scientists predict that nanobots could be outfitted with an array of tools, including onboard sensors, motors, power supplies, arms for manipulating,

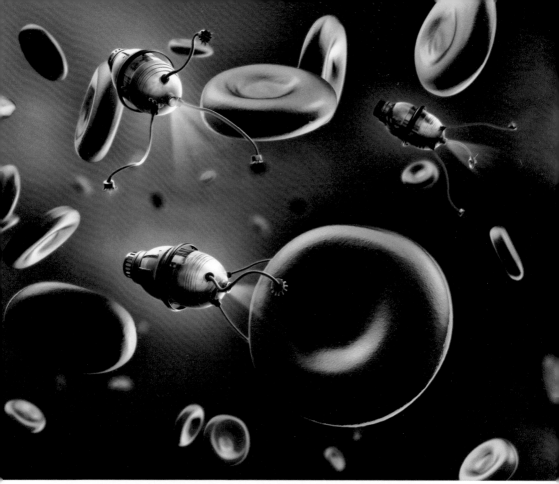

Armies of swimming nanobots might one day become routine surgical tools. Researchers are trying to develop nanobots that can treat tumors or blood clots, repair damaged cells, and deliver drugs directly to body organs.

and molecular computers. The difficulty is getting the nanoscale components to assemble themselves in the proper sequence. This calls for enormously complex systems that can choose and place parts on the nanoscale like the robot arms on an automobile assembly line. The molecular factory would also have to assemble large numbers of surgical nanobots very rapidly. Researchers believe this could be accomplished with arrays of scanning probe tips, such as those used in atomic force microscopes, all programmed to work in unison.

For now the nanobots engineered for medical use are much less complicated. Often they are nanoparticles that are designed to perform special tasks with some automation. Breakthroughs still require approval by government health agencies, such as the

Food and Drug Administration in the United States. Even when a nanobot is approved as safe, and the drug it will deliver is certified for use, the combination of drug and nanobot has to get the green light. "So you're testing it again in the lab, then on animals, then on people," says Aniket Margarkar, a researcher at the Center for Drug Research at the University of Helsinki in Finland. "From the moment you enter the process it can take eight to 10 years to finish."[24] With progress so slow, it may be quite some time before scientists can create nanobots capable of performing a variety of tasks inside patients. Nevertheless many researchers remain optimistic. Some day in the future it may be commonplace for a person to carry around an army of nanoscale physicians performing health maintenance twenty-four hours a day—checking for clogged arteries, monitoring blood pressure and cholesterol, searching for signs of cancer, delivering drugs when necessary. At that point the doctor will always be in.

Chapter 3

Producing Energy from Tiny Sources

Women and men working in the corporate world often talk about wearing power suits appropriate to their status. Now scientists in South Korea have developed a new fabric via nanotechnology that could form the ultimate power suit—capable of generating electric power on its own. The material, which is flexible and foldable like commonplace cloth, generates electricity from the friction produced by ordinary motion. This is like the static electricity that comes from rubbing a balloon on someone's hair. A person wearing a jacket made from the special fabric only has to move naturally to power an electronic device. The fabric is called a wearable triboelectric nanogenerator. (*Tribo* comes from the Greek word for rubbing; triboelectricity is current generated by friction.) The material

contains a polymer-coated layer of microscopic zinc oxide rods only billionths of a meter in length. Surrounding the zinc oxide on top and bottom are layers of silver-coated cloth. When the fabric twists or bends, the rods rub against the silver, sending electrons into the polymer layer. A wire from the so-called smart clothing conducts the electric current, enough to power a cell phone or a blood pressure monitor. Sang-Woo Kim and his team at Sungkyunkwan University in Suwon, South Korea, hope to include batteries to store the power generated by their power suits. Meanwhile they are pleased that their nanogenerator fabric, while a bit heavy, is comfortable for everyday use. Kim insists, "It feels like an ordinary jacket."[25]

A scientist in China blows on a triboelectric generator as part of a demonstration of how the device might be used for harvesting electric current. Energy production is one of the goals of nanotechnology research.

Energy Effects at the Nanoscale

The South Korean team's nanogenerator clothing is just one small example of the effect nanotechnology could have on the world's energy future. In fact, energy production is a field in which nanotechnology stands ready to make an impact very soon. The late Nobel laureate Richard E. Smalley, who worked in nanotechnology at Rice University's Smalley-Curl Institute, identified five grand challenges that civilization faces in the next fifty years: energy, water, environment, disease, and education, with energy production the most crucial. Smalley was convinced that science—and particularly nanotechnology research—can solve these problems. As Smalley advised his students and colleagues, "Others can work on the easy [problems in science], the applied problems. Focus on the grand challenges, the holy grails in nanotechnology. Don't be distracted by the other things!"[26]

One solution that Smalley introduced is called armchair quantum wire. It addresses the fact that the copper-wire electric grid in the United States is estimated to leak electricity at a rate of 5 percent per 100 miles (161 km) of transmission. Since power plants often deliver power to remote locations, the waste can be significant. Smalley proposed replacing copper wire with a weave of metallic nanotubes, each fifty thousand times smaller than a human hair, that could move electricity over long distances with little loss of power. These single-walled carbon nanotubes, called armchairs because of their unusual shape, proved hard to produce in sufficient quantities. However, a Rice University team led by chemist Andrew R. Barron has discovered a way to take individual nanotubes in small batches and dramatically increase their length. They hope to develop a sort of casting furnace that can grow nanotubes from scratch and amplify them into long fibers for power cables. "What we've done is a baby step," says Barron's assistant Alvin Orbaek. "But it verifies that, in the big picture, armchair quantum wire is technically feasible."[27]

There is a worldwide quest today for clean, reliable sources of energy that will help reduce greenhouse gases and meet climate goals. Nanotechnology can play a vital role in this quest, since many effects related to energy production occur at the nanoscale. For example, solar cells use photons from sunlight to unlock electrons from silicon material, channeling the electrons into an electric current. Fuel cells also release electrons and funnel them through an external circuit. Scientists are working on ways to use nanotechnology to make these processes more efficient. As with the armchair quantum wire, small improvements in how things operate can lead to much more efficient energy production and transmission. For example, one drawback to generating power with small wind turbines has been their low energy efficiency. Eagle Windpower Oy, a Finnish company, has developed an improved windmill blade using carbon nanotubes bound by a special epoxy. The new blades are about 50 percent lighter than competitors' fiberglass blades.

The lighter weight allows for increased blade size, which in turn makes the turbines more efficient. According to Juha Siitonen, Eagle's managing director, "Our blades can produce more energy and start operating at low wind speeds. . . . The material enables the doubling of the station's wing size and an increase in power production of 30 percent, when compared to traditional small wind power stations."[28] Since carbon nanotubes are one hundred times stronger than steel, the Eagle blades are also more durable for long-term use. Such innovations on a tiny scale can result in large energy savings.

Revolutionary Solar Steam

Energy savings could also result from a new nanotechnology that helps convert solar energy into steam. Scientists at Rice University in Houston, Texas, are working on a method of using light-capturing nanoparticles to turn sunlight into heat. When the nanoparticles are submerged in water and then exposed to sunlight, they heat up rapidly, vaporizing the water to create steam. The solar steam technology already displays an energy efficiency rate of about 24 percent, but scientists believe this can be increased. By comparison, ordinary solar panels have an efficiency rate of only 15 percent. Oara Neumann, a Rice graduate student and researcher, has videotaped a demonstration of just how effective the solar steam technique can be. Neumann submerged a test tube of water filled with light-activated nanoparticles into a tub of ice water. Then she focused sunlight onto the mixture using a lens, producing steam from nearly frozen water. Such capabilities suggest an alternative to industrial methods of producing steam in giant boilers. "Solar steam is remarkable because of its efficiency," says Neumann. "It does not require acres of

A Nanoreporter for Fossil Fuels

Much of the energy-related research in nanotechnology is geared toward renewable sources such as solar panels and hydrogen fuel cells. However, nanoscale inventions can also impact the fossil fuel industry in positive ways. For example, scientists at Rice University have created a nanoscale detector that can determine the presence and concentration level of hydrogen sulfide in natural gas and crude oil while they are still in the ground. Hydrogen sulfide, which is inherent in natural gas and crude oil, produces a characteristic smell of rotten eggs. The human nose can quickly become desensitized to the gas and unable to detect the higher concentrations that can be fatal. Crude oil with as little as 1 percent hydrogen sulfide is so-called sour crude—toxic and capable of corroding pipelines and storage vessels. The steps to turn sour to sweet crude are expensive. The nanoreporter developed by the chemists James Tour, Michael Wong, and Mason Tomson at Rice lets drillers assess the quality of natural gas and crude oil. The nanoreporter employs tiny carbon particles whose fluorescent properties change when exposed to hydrogen sulfide. Once the particles are pumped out of a production well, they can be analyzed with a spectrometer to find the precise level of contamination. As Wong notes, "Just having information about the sulfur content may be enough to tell a company, 'Let's cap this well and move on to a cheaper site.'"

Quoted in Mike Williams, "Nanoreporters Tell 'Sour' Oil from 'Sweet,'" *Rice News*, April 22, 2014. http://news .rice edu.

mirrors or solar panels. In fact, the footprint can be very small."[29] Because of this small footprint (the amount of space needed for the technology), solar steam could be ideal for use in developing countries with shortages of electric power. Engineering students at Rice have created an autoclave (a pressurized container for sterilizing surgical and dental instruments) that uses solar steam. Naomi Halas, director of Rice's Laboratory for Nanophotonics, is working on a grant project to develop solar-steam methods for treating human waste in economically depressed areas. She and her colleagues also are exploring hybrid heating and air conditioning systems that run on solar steam in daylight and electricity at night to lower costs and save energy.

Nanotechnology for Fuel Cells

Nanotechnology can also lower costs for hydrogen fuel cells, a potential power source for cell phone towers, electric cars, and many other items. Fuel cells generate electricity through a chemical reaction involving hydrogen, the most common element in the universe. On one side of the fuel cell, hydrogen flows through a channel into the anode electrode, where a catalyst splits the hydrogen into positive ions and negatively charged electrons. On the other side, oxygen flows into the cathode electrode. A special membrane in the middle lets only the positively charged ions flow through to the cathode and forces the electrons to detour to the cathode by way of an external circuit, where the electricity is created. The waste product of the fuel cell is plain, environmentally safe water. Hydrogen fuel cells would seem to be an excellent source of energy, but they tend to be expensive. They require platinum or other precious metals as a catalyst to strip off electrons in one electrode and reduce oxygen to water in the other.

That is where nanotechnology can make a difference. James P. Zheng, a professor at the Center for Advanced Power Systems at Florida State University in Tallahassee, has proposed using a nanomaterial that will greatly reduce the amount of platinum included in each fuel cell. The material is called buckypaper, which is the invention of Dr. Ben Wang, a professor of industrial engineering at Florida State. Buckypaper gets its name from the buckyball or Carbon 60 molecule. It is formed from carbon nanotubes that are synthesized into a thin film, stacked, and compressed, making a conductive substance that is ten times lighter than steel but two hundred and fifty times stronger. Zheng found that when buckypaper is combined with platinum in a fuel cell's membrane-electrode assembly, the hydrogen flow is improved and the catalysts work more effectively. Just as important, adding buckypaper to the assembly requires 70 percent less platinum, lowering costs significantly. In 2010 Florida State signed a licensing deal with Bing Energy to manufacture the buckypaper fuel cells. China Telecom is already replacing lead-acid batteries in many of its remote cell phone towers with the new Bing fuel cells. Bing officials tout the buckypaper fuel cell as smaller, lighter, quieter, and less expensive than its competitors. With an estimated 5 million cell phone towers worldwide, the sales opportunity in the telecom area alone is enormous. As for Zheng, he has discovered that buckypaper, with its ability to conduct heat or electricity with ease, has many potential uses. "There are 50 to 60 patents in the United States on Dr. Zheng's buckypaper work," says John Fraser, executive director of the Florida State University Office of Commercialization. "Dr. Zheng is a superstar at FSU, and we have high hopes for him and this technology."[30]

Florida State University's Ben Wang (pictured) invented buckypaper, a nanomaterial that is being used in research to improve hydrogen fuel cell design and efficiency. A microscopic view of buckypaper appears on Wang's computer screen.

Graphene and the Challenge of Hydrogen Storage

Scientists long have harbored high hopes for using hydrogen as a clean, reliable fuel for vehicles. Hydrogen is lightweight and abundant, and produces no toxic emissions, only water vapor and heat. A major drawback to hydrogen, however, is storage and transport. There are three ways hydrogen can be stored: as a compressed gas in heavy metallic high-pressure tanks, as a liquid

Nanofibers Sucking Carbon from the Air

Concerns about climate change are based on the large amount of carbon dioxide pumped into the atmosphere from coal plants, factories, automobiles, and other sources. Now a research group at George Washington University in Washington, DC, is proposing an electrochemical process to recapture that carbon and turn it into carbon nanofibers for building materials and other uses. Currently carbon nanofibers, for all their potential to form strong, lightweight materials, are very expensive to produce. The George Washington group believes the new process could create carbon nanofibers more efficiently and cheaply than existing techniques.

Their method employs molten lithium carbonate with lithium oxide, a related compound, dissolved in it. The lithium oxide binds to carbon dioxide in the air, creating more lithium carbonate. Applying voltage across two electrodes sunk in the molten carbonate produces a reaction with the following byproducts: oxygen, carbon deposits on one of the electrodes, and lithium oxide. The lithium oxide can then capture more carbon dioxide and resume the process. The deposits form carbon nanofibers in different shapes and diameters according to the amount and timing of the voltage. The result is less carbon in the atmosphere and more nanoscale carbon fibers for a variety of uses. According to science writer Mike Orcutt, the George Washington researchers "calculate that given an area less than 10 percent of the size of the Sahara Desert, the method could remove enough carbon dioxide to make global atmospheric levels return to preindustrial levels within 10 years."

Mike Orcutt, "Researcher Demonstrates How to Suck Carbon from the Air, Make Stuff from It," *MIT Technology Review,* August 19, 2015. www.technologyreview.com.

in tanks at a dangerously cold -253° C (-423.4° F), and as a solid mixed with metals or chemical compounds. For hydrogen to be practical as an automotive fuel, of course, its onboard storage must be comparable to that for gasoline—lightweight, safe, compact, and cost-effective. None of the commercial storage solutions have so far been able to satisfy all of the auto industry's strict requirements, leaving hydrogen to languish as a replacement for fossil fuels. That may change, however, due to the promise of nanomaterials for hydrogen storage.

In 2010 Javad Rafiee, an Iranian-born doctoral student at the Rensselaer Polytechnic Institute in Troy, New York, won a $30,000 prize for his creation of a unique form of graphene for hydrogen storage. Graphene, which was discovered in 2004, is essentially a one-atom-thick, tightly packed sheet of carbon atoms bonded in a hexagonal honeycomb pattern. This nanomaterial is the thinnest compound known to science, has a tensile strength one hundred to three hundred times greater than steel, and also conducts heat and electricity to an amazing degree. Jesus de La Fuente, the CEO of a company that develops and markets the material, expresses the opinion of many scientists when he declares that graphene "is as versatile a material as any discovered on Earth."[31] In his prize-winning research, Rafiee subjected graphene to several steps, including mechanical grinding and a heat treatment called annealing, to produce a form uniquely suited to storing hydrogen as fuel. The surface chemistry of Rafiee's graphene, based on the idea that hydrogen tends to cluster around carbon atoms, binds hydrogen to the graphene at room temperature and at low pressure, creating an ideal medium for storage.

Researchers at the University of Maryland believe they can improve on graphene's already high level of storage capacity. Using computer modeling, they have designed a method to fold graphene into a three-dimensional box suitable for hydrogen storage. They have dubbed their method hydrogenation-assisted graphene origami, or HAGO. Hydrogenation means to treat with hydrogen, and origami is the Japanese art of folding paper into decorative shapes from nature. The process begins with a sheet of graphene cut to a precise pattern to form a box. The graphene pattern then actually assembles itself into a three-dimensional box made of carbon atoms, to which hydrogen can become attached for storage. An electric field causes the graphene box to unfold, releasing the hydrogen. "Upon turning off the electric field, the graphene folds up into a box spontaneously again," says Teng Li, a mechanical engineering professor at the university. "Such a process can be repeated many times."[32] His team's origami boxes have proven to be remarkably stable and can store hydrogen at a capacity far in excess of US Department of Energy targets. Perhaps atomic-scale origami will be an important boost for hydrogen-powered cars in the future.

Clean Energy with the Help of Viruses

Even further in the future, abundant clean energy may come from a battery powered by a virus. Most people connect viruses—tiny infectious agents that reproduce themselves inside living cells—with human illness or computer malfunctions, but Angela Belcher, a nanotech scientist at MIT, sees them as remarkably versatile little organisms. For one thing, viruses adapt well to innovations on the molecular scale since they are already of similar size. They align themselves geometrically into very thin films. As living things, their genetic code can be altered to create desirable structures.

And with their ability to reproduce themselves in huge numbers, there is no limit to their supply. Nonscientists might shudder at the thought of vast armies of virus cyborgs, but Belcher insists that making useful things from the simplest life forms on earth is little different from nature's bottom-up and billion-years project of evolution. "We're letting biology help us work on solving . . . what the next next-generation batteries are going to be," she says.[33]

Belcher and her team begin by synthesizing a virus called M13, which is found swarming all over humans but is harmless to them. The M13 virus is engineered to a wire shape about nine nanometers thin. The virus is then made to coat itself with iron phosphate

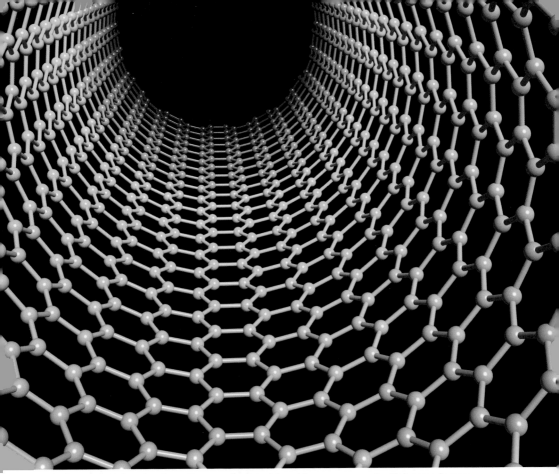

Carbon nanotubes (such as the one depicted here) have many potential uses. In one research project, scientists are using viruses and carbon nanotubes to build new types of high-performance batteries.

and bind to carbon nanotubes, forming a battery cathode that is extremely conductive. According to Belcher, 10 grams (0.35 oz.) of the virus cathode materials can power a portable media player for almost forty hours, equaling the performance of three ordinary portable batteries for a media device. During the assembly process, the virus is no longer alive and cannot reproduce itself. Belcher calls it "a protein scaffold to grab ions out of solution or build materials exactly the way we need them to grow."[34] Her team has also made a battery anode out of viruses coated with cobalt oxide and gold to form tiny wires. Belcher's battery with virus electrodes is one of three innovative viral devices she has invented. Her other devices are a virus fuel cell that harvests hydrogen from water molecules and a virus-nanotube solar cell.

Belcher is convinced that important breakthroughs in energy production are possible from thinking small and combining nanotechnology with nature's own processes.

Meeting the World's Demand for Energy

Researchers like Angela Belcher ensure that nanotechnology will play a vital role in meeting the world's increasing demand for clean, reliable sources of energy. The United Nations estimates that by 2030 global demand for energy will have grown 70 percent since the year 2000. Worldwide funding for nanotech energy projects continues to expand. Nanotechnology solutions can also make solar cells and fuel cells more efficient. In the future scientists will increasingly look to innovations on the nanoscale to solve problems related to energy.

Chapter 4

Warfare on the Nanoscale

Authors from H.G. Wells to J.K. Rowling have described the advantages of being invisible. Modern science has yet to produce a serum for disappearing or an invisibility cloak like the one employed by Harry Potter. However, scientists at MIT have developed the next best thing: a new military uniform made of nanoparticles that deflect light and enable soldiers to blend into their surroundings like an army of chameleons. The MIT research, funded by a five-year, $50 million government grant in 2002, proved so successful that the US Army took over the program and classified it as top secret. The nanoparticles embedded in uniforms can be programmed to bend or reflect light at will. "One of the biggest revolutionary advances we are looking at is chameleonic camouflage," says Jean-Louis DeGay, spokesperson for the Army's Natick Soldier Center in Massachusetts. "Nanotechnology gives us the ability to either change a camouflage pattern in a textile in a moment's notice or even create a mirrored effect."[35] Scientists say one of the inspirations for the nanomaterial in the new uniform was the alien creature in the 1987 movie *Predator*. It could alter its battle suit to bend light or exactly mirror its surroundings, rendering itself virtually invisible. Theoretically the same approach with nanoparticles could also be used on a larger scale to cloak a helicopter or a battleship.

Uniforms like a Second Skin

Invisibility is only one of the features scientists foresee for military uniforms of the future engineered with nanotechnology. One cutting-edge idea, dubbed Second Skin, is a nanotube-based fabric able to repel chemical and biological agents. Scientists at the University of Massachusetts Amherst are developing the fabric in conjunction with the US Defense Threat Reduction Agency. They believe that military uniforms made from the fabric could be deployed in the field in less than a decade. The fabric is designed to switch back and forth from a highly breathable state to a more protective one in response to a chemical or biological threat. Like a smart second skin, it will respond to the environment to protect its wearer, with no need for outside control.

The fabric's lightweight breathable quality comes from membranes with pores made of vertically aligned carbon nanotubes. This increases the wearer's comfort and safety in hot environments that might also be contaminated. The carbon layer is overlaid with a surface layer designed to respond to chemical warfare agents. Sensors cause the fabric to switch to a protective state by closing off the pores or by sloughing off the contaminated surface layer. Since biological agents such as bacteria and viruses are about ten nanometers in size, the uniform's membrane pores, which are only a few nanometers wide, are able to block them. When faced with chemical agents in smaller particles, such as mustard gas and nerve gas, the carbon nanotube membranes are able to respond by closing the pores and blocking the threat like tiny gatekeepers. Scientists are now working on a shedding response in which the fabric will react to anthrax spores or nerve agents by sloughing off contaminated areas like real skin. The carbon layer and membrane are manufactured by bringing together nanoparticles and polymers to create highly functional materials. Manufacture of the membranes and carbon layers is carried out in the university's Roll-to-Roll Nanofabrication Laboratory. Scientists on the project believe nanotechnology can be a boon to the nation's soldiers. According to Tracee Harris, technology manager at the Defense Threat Reduction Agency, "This futuristic uniform would allow our military forces to operate safely for extended time periods and successfully complete their missions in environments contaminated with chemical and biological agents."[36]

Body Armor in Liquid and Foam

Another safety measure for soldiers of the future is sophisticated body armor. Here again the unusual properties of nanotechnology offer surprising possibilities for the future. For example, a mixture resembling motor oil or maple syrup might seem a poor candidate for stopping a bullet. Yet liquid body armor promises to be more effective than Kevlar (a synthetic fiber) in protecting a wearer from bullets and other projectiles. The proper term for liquid body armor is actually *shear-thickening fluid* (STF), a substance first developed in 2002 at the US Army Research Laboratory in Adelphi, Maryland. STF consists of silica nanoparticles suspended in liquid polymers. STF ordinarily behaves like a liquid, allowing a soldier wearing it inside protective clothing to flex and move about easily. However, when exposed to the stress of a projectile, the substance hardens to a solid within milliseconds.

Scientists are trying to design a carbon nanotube fabric that will protect wearers from deadly anthrax spores (visible through a scanning electron micrograph). If successful, projects such as this could protect members of the military who are subjected to chemical warfare.

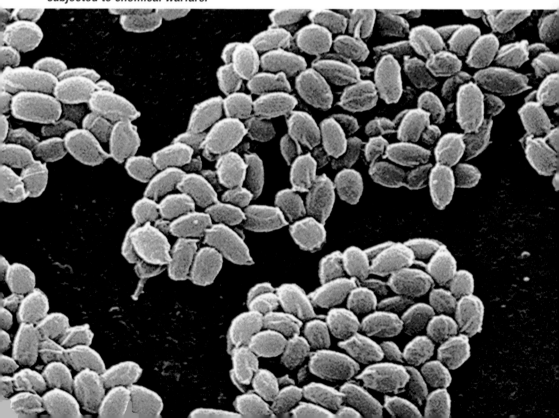

This is because the energy of a ballistic strike on the material causes the nanoparticles to assemble into temporary hydroclusters, which are long chains of molecules in irregular shapes. The hydroclusters then overlap into a strong, meshlike structure, increasing the viscosity to a solid state. When the energy from the projectile stress is gone, the process works in reverse and the STF goes back to a liquid state.

WORDS IN CONTEXT

hydroclusters
Particles that are momentarily compressed together to form irregular long chains.

Military scientists plan to add STF to Kevlar to make body armor that is stronger and more flexible for combat missions. Typically twenty to forty layers of Kevlar are required for effective body armor, making a stiff shell that hinders ordinary movement. With STF treatment added, only about four layers of Kevlar are needed. Due to the STF's improved ability to dissipate a bullet's impact over a wider area and restrict its depth of penetration, it also reduces the wearer's pain from a bullet strike. And body armor is only one of STF's many possible functions. Its rigidness upon sudden impact or pressure makes it an ideal material for the soles of paratroopers' jump boots or surgeons' gloves subject to scalpel slices or needle pricks. STF could even be used as a quick fix for potholes on damaged roads.

The US Army is also investigating the use of extremely lightweight nanofoam for protective body armor. Structural engineer Yu Qiao and his team at the University of California, San Diego, have developed a process for creating nanofoam by mixing together two substances at the molecular level and then using acid etching or combustion to remove one of the materials. This leaves behind the desired foam material with tiny empty pores like a sponge caused by the removal of the targeted substance. The key to the nanofoam's effectiveness is the size of those pores. Ranging in tests from just ten nanometers across to ten microns, the tiny pores enable the nanofoam to absorb the impact energy of a projectile over a wider area, greatly increasing its resistance. In fact Qiao and his colleagues have found that the smaller ten-nanometer pores make for the best performance. "[The nanofoams] will appear to be less

The Institute for Soldier Nanotechnologies

In 2002 the US Army embarked on one of the largest research programs in modern history. The Institute for Soldier Nanotechnologies (ISN), located at MIT, began as a five-year, $50 million commitment to research nanoscale solutions for military needs. The ISN, housed in a new twenty-eight-thousand square foot campus center, comprised a staff of one hundred fifty research scientists, including forty-four members of the MIT faculty from eight different departments. It also drew upon several industrial partners, including DuPont, Raytheon, and Dow Corning. It originally focused on three main areas of research: protections against gunshots and bioweapons, performance enhancement, and injury prevention and treatment. One program, called the Objective Force Warrior, sought to incorporate nanotechnology into an integrated combat system for individual soldiers. According to a 2009 MIT report, "The ultimate goal [of the ISN] is to help the Army create a 21st-century battlesuit that combines high-tech protection and survivability capabilities with low weight and increased comfort."

In recent years the ISN's staff and resources have been scaled back. As in other research areas, military use of nanotechnology has proven to be a more difficult project than originally thought. Yet promising research is still going forward. For example, a recent joint venture between the ISN and MIT scientists produced a combat uniform that incorporates gold microfibers that enable a soldier to detect heat, light, and sound. The fibers also enable soldiers to communicate with each other simply by speaking into their uniforms.

Quoted in Institute for Soldier Nanotechnologies, *MIT Reports to the President 2009–2010*. http://web.mit.edu.

rigid," explains Qiao, "but will actually be more resistant than ordinary foams."[37] He hopes that nanofoam can someday be employed in headgear to protect soldiers from brain trauma injuries. On a much larger scale, nanofoam could also protect entire buildings from bomb blasts and shrapnel.

Smart Uniforms with Nanosensors

With the help of nanosensors, military uniforms of the future could protect soldiers in many other ways. Nanosensors are carbon nanotubes, nanowires, or particles that collect and convey data on the nanoscale. One application employs these sensors to trigger nanomaterials to become rigid or form synthetic "muscle." Mechanical engineers and chemists at MIT's Institute for Soldier Nanotechnologies have experimented with materials made from polymers that react to electrical signals and become rigid on command. For a soldier who has fallen and broken a leg, nanosensors would stiffen the material into a hardened form, immobilizing the limb like a cast. Rapid loss of blood from a gunshot wound in the arm or leg would trigger sensors to harden the material and constrict blood flow near the wound like a tourniquet. Such exomuscles might also be activated to provide soldiers with superhuman strength or extraordinary jumping ability, a nanotech version of the movies' Iron Man (and suitable for iron women in the military as well). Uniforms with nanosensors could monitor soldiers' physiological condition in real time. When deploying personnel, commanders could access precise data about each soldier's heart rate, blood pressure, level of hydration, and chemical signs of stress, such as exhaling increased nitric oxide. Nanosensors could also create a so-called electronic nose, programmed to detect biological or chemical agents in toxic gases and vapors. These sensors would employ nanowires made from submicrometer layers of different metals, including gold, silver, and nickel. They would be able to detect different pathogens, such as anthrax, smallpox, and ricin, by identifying their unique fluorescent traits. All these features, along with an onboard computer and weapons enhanced by nanotech, could theoretically be included in a uniform system weighing no more than 120 pounds (54.4 kg), the acceptable burden for three days of active duty. As Henry Everitt of US Army Research has said, "Nanotech will be pervasive in the military of the future. It has to be."[38]

Smart Dust for Surveillance

Nanotechnology could also help soldiers of the future track the movements of enemy forces. In the last hundred years military surveillance tools have shrunk from hot-air balloons and supersonic aircraft to drones no larger than a microwave oven. Within

Computer artwork depicting a nanomachine clinging to a dust mote illustrates the idea behind smart dust. Machines the size of dust particles could one day be used by the military to relay precise information in a war zone.

twenty years a commando team seeking to flush out pockets of resistance in a war-torn city might employ a new kind of surveillance tool: smart dust. The commando team leader would release portable packets of nanosensors like dust particles that float in the air throughout the city. The smart dust sensors would circulate freely in the city, covering areas such as tight alleyways and cul-de-sacs that even small drones would have difficulty reaching. The nanosensors would relay up-to-the-second information, including GPS readings of enemy movements, biometric data

Ethical Concerns About Military Nanotechnology

Today all the major powers of the world are developing military uses for nanotechnology. The United States is among the most aggressive, approaching nanotechnology as a crucial field of research. The aim is not weapons of mass destruction, like the atomic bomb of the Manhattan Project; instead, much of the work seeks ways to use nanotech to protect soldiers from attack and enable them to engage the enemy with less risk. Panicked predictions about nanotechnology being used to create doomsday devices, such as bombs that pollute enemy airspace with microbe-like nanomachines, have not come to pass.

Nonetheless critics question the ethics of military research on nanotechnology. Many fear that the technological and engineering superiority enjoyed by the United States and other large powers could result in more fighting rather than less. As one side's nanoenhanced soldiers become almost invulnerable on the battlefield—or soldiers operate remote-controlled weapons from a keyboard at a safe distance—commanders may resort to force more readily than they would have done otherwise. At the same time, forces outgunned by nanotechnology may turn to violence against an enemy's civilian population, leading to more deaths from terrorism. "One significant downside of invulnerability, then, is that one's enemies will attack one's compatriots, who *are* vulnerable," observe Robert Simpson and Robert Sparrow, professors of international studies at Monash University in Melbourne, Australia. For all its promise of reducing battlefield casualties, nanotechnology actually raises many new ethical questions about the legitimate tactics of war.

Quoted in Bert Gordijn and Anthony Mark Cutter, eds., *In Pursuit of Nanoethics: Transatlantic Reflections on Nanotechnology.* Netherlands: Springer, 2014, p. 99.

(biological statistics about individuals), temperature changes, chemical breakdowns, and countless other data sets. Soldiers would receive the data on helmets equipped with heads-up display (HUD) screens, enabling them to react instantly to snipers, saboteurs, or biochemical threats lurking around the corner.

The military use of smart dust proceeds from the idea of the Internet of Things—a network of objects connected by sensors, software, and other electronics. It is already feasible to link many of the information-gathering devices in the world on a network, including things like security and traffic cameras, satellites, weather balloons, and car sensors, in order to send a constant flow of information through the Internet to be collected on a database. Such a network could provide a way to monitor almost anything. Smaller and smaller sensors could be scattered everywhere—on buildings, on roads and vehicles, and in border areas—to increase the monitoring potential. Smart dust would be the ultimate surveillance network, employing sensors the size of dust motes to form an information-gathering network able to encompass large areas with great precision.

The concept of smart dust began with a joint research project by the Defense Advanced Research Projects Agency (DARPA) and the RAND Corporation in the 1990s. Scientists created smart dust from individual "motes," or microscopic sensors equipped to perform a number of functions. One smart dust mote can contain a semiconductor laser diode, a microsystem for transmitting and receiving images, circuitry for processing control signals, and a power source based on special batteries and solar cells. The tiny size of these microelectronic wonders is made possible by advances in digital circuitry. The ultimate goal is to deploy smart dust as a rapid, widespread wireless network of linked sensors, able to operate in the chaos of a war zone. Like many breakthroughs in military technology, smart dust could also be adapted easily to civilian use. Packets of smart dust could be sprayed on farmland to monitor crops and prevent infestation or spread in forests to study animal migration patterns and tree growth. In fact, science writer Dan Rowinski sees the nonmilitary uses of smart dust as even more exciting. "It is much more fascinating to imagine planetary exploration: using Dust to monitor the environmental conditions of potentially habitable worlds," says Rowinski. "Or to monitor the inner processes of the human brain. . . . The world may soon be quantified by sensors, floating on the winds to everywhere."[39]

Nanothermite and Mininukes

It is not that large a step from microscopic sensors to bombs made with microscopic particles. Nanotechnology is already being used to create compact explosives called nanothermites that are ten times more powerful than conventional bombs. The metallic nanoparticles they contain offer more surface area in contact with the particles of the various chemicals that make up the explosive. Once a chemical reaction begins, setting off the explosion, the greater surface area of the nanoparticles produces a more rapid reaction rate and a much more powerful explosion. Weapons designers can change the size of the nanoparticles to control the release rate of energy, enabling them to customize nanothermite bombs for different uses. US Air Force scientists, for example, have found that aluminum nanoparticles are particularly effective in nanothermites. These bombs are small yet very powerful, making them ideal for use with remote-controlled drones.

Breakthroughs in nanotechnology "could completely change the face of weaponry," says Andy Oppenheimer, a weapons expert with the analyst firm Jane's Information Group.[40] Oppenheimer notes that the United States, Germany, and Russia are performing research on so-called mininukes—nuclear explosives created with the aid of nanotechnology. These devices could employ superlasers to trigger relatively small thermonuclear fusion explosions equivalent to a ton or a few hundred tons of high explosives. This type of mininuke device would weigh only a few kilograms and comfortably fit into a backpack or briefcase. Since it would include very little or no fissionable material (material used in nuclear fission), it would produce almost no radioactive fallout. Due to its comparatively small explosive power, such a mininuke would also fall outside the legal constraints of nuclear nonproliferation treaties.

Many scientists and military experts worry about the destructive possibilities of weaponry based on nanotechnology. For example, the scaled-down explosiveness of a mininuke might make it more likely to be used. Some experts question the ethics of research on such devices. "The creation of much smaller nuclear bombs adds new challenges to the effort to limit weapons of mass destruction," Oppenheimer warns. "[The bombs] could blow open everything that is in place for arms control. . . . Everything gets more dangerous."[41]

Nanotech for Less Lethal Weapons

Nanotechnology can also help produce weapons that are less lethal than those of the past. In November 2014 the US Navy deployed a nanotech Laser Weapon System on the USS *Ponce* that has adjustable levels of power from stun up to kill. The laser also has the capability of disabling a targeted aircraft with limited force instead of destroying it. "The [international] law currently does not require such gradual application of force," observes technology expert Hitoshi Nasu. "However, it could well be adopted as government policy for a specific operation from political or ethical considerations."[42] Nanosensors are another technology that can help reduce the lethal nature of powerful weapons. Nanosensors on board the miniaturized Hummingbird Nano Air Vehicle (NAV) can hit targets with incredible precision, reducing or avoiding civilian casualties even more effectively than drones. The Hummingbird, which is shaped like its namesake, is about 15 centimeters (5.9 in.) long and weighs just 19 grams (0.67 oz.). It is designed for urban missions, due to its unique ability to operate within crowds or even inside buildings. Nanotechnology helps equip the Hummingbird with tiny motors, batteries, flight controls, communication systems, and a video camera for surveillance. Another result of nanotechnology research is the nonlethal smart bullet. SmartRounds Technology of Brighton, Colorado, created the bullets to employ Micro-Electro-Mechanical Systems (MEMS) technology. Each bullet is equipped with two solid-state microsensors that are turned on when the round is fired and activate the smart bullet milliseconds before impact. One smart bullet, called the ShockRound, produces a sudden flash-bang and a shock wave of nitrogen gas that disables the targeted assailant. Another, the PepperRound, explodes in a flash-bang and cloud of capsaicin (the active ingredient in chili peppers), rendering the assailant helpless due to a burning sensation in the eyes and throat.

The miniaturized Hummingbird drone is equipped with tiny motors, batteries, flight controls, and communications systems made possible through nanotechnology. Nanosensors can also help it hit targets with incredible precision.

Futurists have often described doomsday scenarios in which toxic nanoparticles become the ultimate weapon, invading the human body like swarming bacteria. However, defense scientists in the United States and elsewhere are intent on finding ways to use nanotechnology to limit lethal violence in warfare. Each society will decide which version of the technology wins out over the coming years and decades.

Chapter 5

A World-Changing Technology

On the 1980s science fiction show *Star Trek: The Next Generation,* Captain Jean-Luc Picard, in the mood for relaxation, would request a machine to make his favorite beverage: Earl Grey tea. The replicator, as the device was called, could produce almost any nonliving object, from food to spare parts to deadly weapons. It supposedly worked by rearranging subatomic particles into different molecular structures. Today some scientists insist that a technology much like the replicator is not only possible but perhaps lies only a couple of decades away. They believe nanotechnology promises a similar method of assembling things from the bottom up, atom by atom. Charles Sykes, a professor of chemistry at Tufts University near Boston, Massachusetts, notes that nature itself offers a perfect model for recombining atoms and molecules in wondrous ways. "Life itself is not possible without the multitude of molecular machines inside our bodies that work in turbulent environments and with very little power but accomplish very complex tasks from virus transport to muscle flexing," says Sykes. "Many wonderful things are possible as nature has already proven."[43]

The Ultimate Form of Nanotechnology

The ability to imitate nature by manipulating atoms and molecules is the ultimate form of nanotechnology—the holy grail of researchers and theorists. The idea goes back to American physicist Richard Feynman's visionary 1959 lecture "There's Plenty of Room at the Bottom," in which he suggested that objects and devices could one day be assembled to specifications on the atomic scale. "The principles of physics, as far as I can see,"

Feynman observed in his talk, "do not speak against the possibility of maneuvering things atom by atom. It is not an attempt to violate any laws; it is something, in principle, that can be done."[44]

Through the years, and inspired in part by Feynman's vision, scientists and engineers have developed methods to see atoms more clearly and move them with more precision than ever before. Problems of size—the discrepancy between the scale of ordinary visual reality and the atomic world—have been addressed with great success. Matter on the nanoscale is now the province of everyday science, as shown by the fabrication of carbon nanotubes for building materials and the use of nanotechnology in products ranging from sunscreen to golf clubs. Feynman's ideas about creating nanoscale electric circuits are already being realized in research labs around the world. With these facts in mind, it is obvious that his notion of manufacturing things atom by atom using billions of microscopic factories is no longer so farfetched. Feynman himself knew that some of science's most fanciful ideas have a way of becoming reality.

Atomically Precise Manufacturing

In 1981 K. Eric Drexler, then a research scientist at the Space Systems Laboratory at MIT, showed that he took Feynman's ideas very seriously indeed. Drexler published a landmark paper titled "Molecular Engineering," which outlined a way to carry out the manipulation of molecules. At the start Drexler noted Feynman's basic insight: "[Feynman] suggested that ordinary machines could build smaller machines that could build still smaller machines, working step by step down toward the molecular level."[45] Drexler went on to describe how biochemical systems in nature provide a blueprint for assembling things on the atomic scale. As an example, he cited the complex system of proteins in DNA. The ribosome—a sort of protein assembly line for living creatures—assembles itself from more than fifty different protein molecules, folding together its component parts in a natural process. Drexler

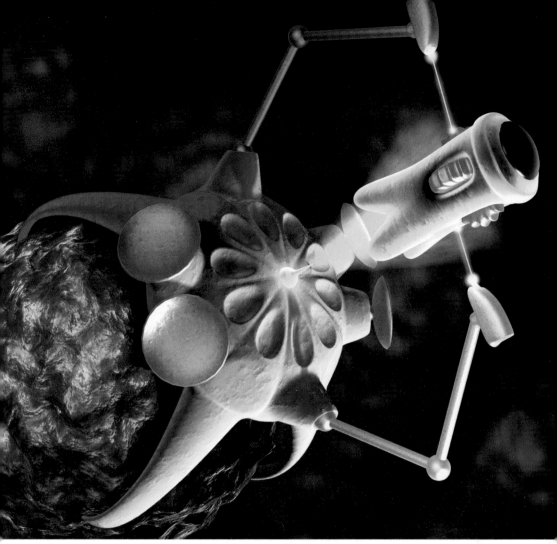

Computer artwork illustrates the concept of self-replicating nanomachines. It shows a nanorobot assembler using a claw to attach itself to a bacterium that will provide the raw materials needed for assembling more nanorobots.

believed it was possible to build molecular machines in a similar way and that these machines could "extend the capabilities of technology many fold in many areas."[46]

He also admitted that such a technology could present to humanity as many dangers (which he did not specify) as opportunities. Nevertheless Drexler thought molecular engineering was inevitable, if not in the short term then certainly in decades to come.

Five years later Drexler refined his ideas in *Engines of Creation: The Coming Era of Nanotechnology.* He proposed creating a nanoscale machine that could move about and assemble copies of

Federal Funding for APM Research

When the US Congress established the National Nanotechnology Initiative (NNI), the future looked bright for federally funded research into nanotechnology. And indeed the NNI grew into a billion-dollar program that supported many aspects of nanotech. Yet some scientists, including K. Eric Drexler, feel betrayed by the NNI. They expected the program to focus on atomically precise manufacturing, with the understanding that APM was its mandated purpose for existing. Drexler points out that the glossy public brochure boosting NNI in 1999 gave this impression. It asked, "What if we could build things the way nature does—atom by atom and molecule by molecule?" A formal plan for the NNI stated that the essence of nanotechnology is the ability to build things at the molecular level. Nonetheless by 2002 NNI's mission had grown (or shrunk) to focus on any research at the nanoscale. Atoms and molecules were scarcely mentioned in newer promotional materials.

One problem was that leading scientists connected with nanotechnology, such as the chemist Richard Smalley, made public statements equating APM with dark fantasies of self-replicating nanobots in profusion—the "grey goo" described in Drexler's first book. At any rate, research on APM met with little support, financial or otherwise, for several years. Drexler reckons that APM research in other countries was also hobbled. Only in the last few years has funding for APM research begun to rebound. "The missing ingredient needed for progress toward APM," says Drexler, "isn't a breakthrough in science, but a breakthrough in purpose and organization."

K. Eric Drexler, *Radical Abundance: How a Revolution in Nanotechnology Will Change Civilization.* New York: Public Affairs, 2013, pp. 204, 211.

itself or other objects of molecular size by steering individual atoms into place. Such a machine could in turn build larger and more complicated structures in a sort of production line on the molecular scale. Also, since Drexler, much like Feynman, enjoys pursuing his notions to their logical extreme, he could not resist describing potentially disastrous consequences for nanotechnology, such as nanobots that could reproduce themselves endlessly at tremendous speed, forming an overwhelming tide of what he called grey goo. Then as now such notions sounded like the wildest science fiction. And since the ability to manufacture things on the atomic scale still did not exist, nanotechnology began to seem like one more overhyped quirk of science. "Do you remember the nanotechnology hype waves in the 90s?" writes tech expert Giulio Prisco. "Nanotechnology—the Next Big Thing—would change the world in only a few years. . . . Tiny machines would re-assemble dirt and waste to build everything that we could dream of, one molecule at a time. And all that was coming, you know, real soon."[47]

Yet some researchers continued to pursue the assembly of things from atoms and molecules as a real possibility. They called it atomically precise manufacturing (APM), the fabrication of goods from the bottom up, atom by atom and molecule by molecule. Prisco compares APM to 3D nanoprinting, like making copies on the atomic scale. "Desktop 3D printers are already able to do very precise and detailed work," says Prisco. "Now imagine a 3D printer able to pick up individual atoms or molecules of whatever material is needed at a given step, and put them in place with atomic precision. . . . APM is visionary but doable, and could be the next technology revolution—this time for real."[48] Several high-profile scientists, including Nicholas Negroponte, one of the founding developers of the Internet, agree that APM and nanomachines are no longer the stuff of fantasy. They believe that nanotechnology might advance like information technology has and could soon produce explosive growth.

In 2013 Drexler surveyed the possibilities for APM in his book *Radical Abundance: How a Revolution in Nanotechnology Will Change Civilization.* Gone were his predictions of nanobot assemblers able to reproduce themselves. Instead he focused on the practical aspects of being able to make fuels, materials, and devices by manipulating molecules. Drexler predicted that APM could result in a massive new abundance of all sorts of products, making them no more expensive than cardboard or aluminum foil. With the advances in nanotechnology that had occurred since his last book twenty-seven years before, Drexler's forecast no longer sounded like science fiction.

Research on the Road to APM

Several examples of practical manufacturing on the nanoscale demonstrate how APM might be carried out. The most obvious one is the manufacture of computer chips. Through a process much like lithographic printing, tiny chips are stamped with patterns of millions or even billions of pixels. Chemical processing then brings out these patterns as contours in a plastic film on a silicon wafer. The patterns are exposed to heat, ion beams, or reactive gases to form them into transistors, insulators, and wires. The patterns are not quite atomically precise—as would be required for effective APM—but chip miniaturization already shows that practical machines and parts can be formed on the atomic scale.

Researchers at IBM are manufacturing tiny 3D transistors using a technique known as directed self-assembly. The IBM team begins with a special class of materials called block copolymers—chains of large molecules consisting of two kinds of blocks, or monomers. By tailoring the polymers' length, size, and other characteristics, scientists can make the blocks attract and repel each other, forming themselves into complex patterns such as densely packed rows. The dense packing enables certain parts of an integrated circuit to be smaller and more efficient than those made with previous methods. "They've used these polymers not just to make pretty patterns but to make some working devices," says Caroline Ross, a materials scientist at MIT conducting research on directed self-assembly. "They've demonstrated a creative way of getting patterns that normally wouldn't form."[49]

Another intriguing project is ongoing at Northwestern University in Evanston, Illinois. Researchers there are using DNA to program nanoparticles to build supercrystals with special optical properties. The supercrystals are hundreds to thousands of times larger than conventional crystals and conduct electricity differently than conventional solids. The scientists first use computer models to predict what light-controlling properties can be created by different crystalline structures. Then they use DNA to place the metal nanoparticles with precise spacing to create supercrystals with the desired properties. With different sizes, shapes, and lattice structures, the crystals can be employed as highly sensitive

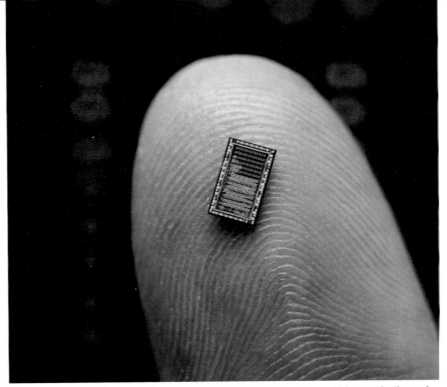

Scientists envision a day when a computer chip (pictured) could be made through atomically precise manufacturing (APM) techniques. Building machines and parts on the atomic scale is the goal of APM.

sensors, lenses, and solar cells and batteries, among other uses. As Northwestern team leader Chad Mirkin explains,

> We usually think of DNA as the genetic blueprint of life, but in this context, however, we have used it to modify nanoparticles so that they can act as "programmable atom equivalents." We can then assemble the nanoparticles into the crystalline architectures we want by making them encounter other particles with complementary sequences. Using our technique we have succeeded in making over 30 different crystal symmetries, five of which do not exist in nature.[50]

Mirkin and the Northwestern group next hope to use DNA programmable assembly to create a mix of materials from nanoparticles. They eventually want to create a vast library of new materials, many of which cannot be found in nature or made with conventional chemistry. At the same time they are demonstrating that precision assembly on the nanoscale is not just possible, it is doable.

Building Blocks of DNA

The DNA molecule is responsible for most of the successful experiments with atomically precise manufacturing so far. It is used not for its ability to carry genetic data but rather for its structural material. DNA's four base proteins bind together strongly or weakly depending on how they are paired along a DNA double helix strand. This enables scientists to change the ways they are joined together, like rearranging building blocks or LEGOs. "The fundamental building blocks of life already have the features required to fold, join, build and grow—so they're perfectly suited to building things at the nano-scale," says science writer Jamie Condliffe. "Geometries are first modeled on computers to work out what molecules are required, then the appropriate ones can be DNA synthesized in order that they can be put together—just like a LEGO kit."[51]

Drexler's idea of nanomachines that can assemble themselves is also borne out by the capabilities of DNA. Since certain base sequences tend to bind together while others do not, DNA molecules can build themselves into extremely complex structures, such as the supercrystals at Northwestern. Ned Seeman's laboratory at New York University has achieved incredibly complex synthetic molecules using DNA-based computation and binding.

Self-assembling nanotech molecules are also able to move on their own. In fact when fueled with the proper chemicals, they can take nanoscale "steps" along a precise path, as shown by researchers at Oxford University. Walking molecules can perform specific tasks, such as moving gold nanoparticles from place to place as tags for optical imaging. Mechanical engineers have also constructed nanoscale motors from molecules. The smallest can whirl about a sulphur atom at speeds up to seventy-two hundred revolutions per minute. The fastest, fashioned from three bulkier molecular parts, can spin at eighteen thousand revolutions per minute, a speed similar to a jet engine. A team of researchers in the Netherlands has made a nanocar from a single molecule. It runs on pulses of electrons, ten of which are required to move the vehicle six nanometers—not exactly a cross-country trip, but impressive nonetheless. Seeman's New York University lab

Dangers of Atomically Precise Manufacturing

Supporters of atomically precise manufacturing predict it could lead to a world of cheap, abundant products, clean energy and water, and freedom from disease. However, critics note that APM presents many possible dangers to human society. For example, the advent of APM could seem brutally sudden to most people, its impact much like that of the Industrial Revolution, only compressed into a few years. The economic upheaval due to a flood of cheap products could bring down governments and spark revolts among citizens. Jobs and careers might become obsolete overnight. If the technology is widely shared, then patent, copyright, and brand protections could be lost in a deluge of cheap copies. Overuse of inexpensive, disposable items could produce a tide of trash and environmental damage. As awareness of these risks increases, there may be calls to ban nanotechnology outright. This raises an even greater danger that one nation, or a group of nations, might gain control of the technology, creating the world's largest monopoly.

Other dangers spring from criminal or terrorist use of APM technology. Chemical and biological weapons employing nanoparticles could be endlessly fabricated and concealed in a pocketed vial. Paranoia about crime or terrorism could lead governments to build networks of self-assembled nanoscale supercomputers, sensors, and weapons. Rulers could turn their countries into virtual prisons. As an editorialist at the Center for Responsible Nanotechnology warns, "An extreme or knee-jerk response to any of these risks will simply create fertile ground for other risks."

"Dangers of Molecular Manufacturing," Center for Responsible Nanotechnology. www.crnano.org.

has even programmed four nanobots to form an assembly line and build a tiny device. The nanobots, tiny machines made from strands of DNA, can walk along a special chemical surface and use their "hands" to pass gold nanoparticles from one to another. They can assemble eight different products with these simple motions. Indeed these innovations, from self-assembling nanomachines to nanoscale motors and transports to a molecular production line, demonstrate the feasibility of tiny factories based on nanotechnology—the beginnings of an industrial revolution on the molecular scale.

A World Changer

The revolution brought about by atomically precise manufacturing could change the world. The ability to nudge atoms into place one by one to form molecules and then larger molecules and then intricate molecular structures of all kinds would open doors to all sorts of technological advances. Computer hardware would reach its ultimate potential, with molecular computers formed from molecular logic gates and connected by molecular wires. According to nanotech researcher Ralph Merkle, "Nanotechnology will let us achieve the ultimate in precision: almost every atom in exactly the right place; make complex and molecularly intricate structures as easily and inexpensively as simple materials; [and] reduce manufacturing costs to little more than the cost of the required raw materials and energy." Merkle adds that nanoscale factories will prob-

Tiny gears inside a micromechanical motor can be seen in this colored scanning electron micrograph. Eventually, motors on the nanoscale may be able to move standard-size objects.

ably use some sort of convergent assembly process in which "vast numbers of small parts are assembled by vast numbers of small robotic arms into larger parts, those larger parts are assembled by larger robotic arms into still larger parts, and so forth."[52] Doubling the size of the parts at each step would enable parts a few atoms in size to become roughly a meter in diameter in only thirty steps. And this self-assembly process need never take a day off.

Should APM become widely available, the result would be, in Drexler's phrase, radical abundance—an endless supply of inexpensive consumer products, materials, foods, and fuels, some perhaps accessible from the home, much like computer downloads today. The pace of change would require new forms of planning and cooperation among people and nations. Economic systems based on the scarcity of raw materials would have to adapt to the new reality. Some theorists believe the APM revolution could free humanity from the age-old struggle to provide food and shelter, leading to new patterns of daily life. "The [nanotechnology] revolution that follows can bring a radical abundance beyond the dreams of any king," Drexler observes, "a post-industrial material abundance that reaches the ends of the earth and lightens its burden."[53]

Atomically precise manufacturing, while seemingly feasible, remains decades away. Yet the benefits of other forms of nanotechnology can already be seen in many areas, including alternative energy, medicine, and agriculture. Until now, nanotechnology has mainly been used to improve products and devices. It can make body armor lighter and harder, solar panels more efficient, sunscreen more protective, and lasers more powerful and more precise. Nanoparticles can monitor the health of the body's tissues and target diseased cells. Nanotechnology might also have dangerous consequences, as with the use of nanosensors for government surveillance or nanoparticles for toxic weapons. As science learns how to manipulate atoms and molecules in new ways, the unseen world on the nanoscale will continue to affect people's lives in unpredictable ways.

> **WORDS IN CONTEXT**
>
> **logic gates**
> Electronic functions that transform an input or inputs into a single logical output.

Source Notes

Introduction: A Miniaturized Surgeon

1. Quoted in Jacopo Prisco, "Will Nanotechnology Soon Allow You to 'Swallow the Doctor'?," CNN, January 30, 2015. www.cnn.com.
2. Quoted in Prisco, "Will Nanotechnology Soon Allow You to 'Swallow the Doctor'?"
3. K. Eric Drexler, *Radical Abundance: How a Revolution in Nanotechnology Will Change Civilization.* New York: Public Affairs, 2013, p. x.

Chapter 1: The History of Nanotechnology

4. Richard Feynman, "There's Plenty of Room at the Bottom," *Nanotechnology—Created by Dr. Ralph Merkle.* www.zyvex.com.
5. Feynman, "There's Plenty of Room at the Bottom."
6. Feynman, "There's Plenty of Room at the Bottom."
7. Quoted in Royal Society of Chemistry, "Feynman's Fancy," January 2009. www.rsc.org.
8. Quoted in Royal Society of Chemistry, "Feynman's Fancy."
9. Lawrence Osborne, "The Grey-Goo Problem," *New York Times*, December 14, 2003. www.nytimes.com.
10. Drexler, *Radical Abundance*, p. 53.
11. "Scanning Tunneling Microscope," *IBM 100*. www-03.ibm.com.
12. Quoted in "Sumio Iijima: Biography," *Engineering and Technology History Wiki.* http://ethw.org.
13. Quoted in Tim Harper, "2015: The Year of the Trillion Dollar Nanotechnology Market?," *AZO Nano*, January 2, 2015. www.azonano.com.

Chapter 2: Surgeons in the Bloodstream

14. Quoted in Nick D'Alto, "A Very Small Surgical Procedure," *Odyssey: Adventures in Science.* http://mazur.harvard.edu.

15. Quoted in D'Alto, "A Very Small Surgical Procedure."

16. Marie Freebody, "Nanosurgery Operates at the Cutting Edge of Medicine," *Biophotonics*. www.photonics.com.

17. Quoted in Freebody, "Nanosurgery Operates at the Cutting Edge of Medicine."

18. Quoted in Daniel Vargas, "Laser Surgery Probe Targets Single Cancer Cells," *UT News,* June 30, 2008. https://news.utexas.edu.

19. Robert Langer, "Nanotechnology and Medicine," *Serious Science*, May 8, 2014. http://serious-science.org.

20. Guizhi Zhu, "Nanomedicine," *The Scientist*, August 1, 2014. www.the-scientist.com.

21. Quoted in "Magnet Nanoparticles Could Be Key to Effective Immunotherapy," *Phys.org*, July 15, 2015. http://phys.org.

22. Feynman, "There's Plenty of Room at the Bottom."

23. Simone Schürle, "Minimally Invasive Eye Surgery on the Horizon as Magnetically Guided Microbots Approach Clinical Trials," *Robohub*, June 26, 2013. http://robohub.org.

24. Quoted in Rose Eveleth, "Why There Aren't Yet Nanobot Doctors," *The Atlantic,* August 6, 2015. www.theatlantic.com.

Chapter 3: Producing Energy from Tiny Sources

25. Quoted in Stephen Ornes, "'Smart' Clothes Generate Electricity," *Student Science,* March 23, 2015. https://student.societyforscience.org.

26. Quoted in "Nanotechnology and Rice University," *Rice University*. http://cnst.rice.edu.

27. Quoted in Darren Quick, "Breakthrough in Development of Cable for Ultra-Efficient Electricity Grid of the Future," *Gizmag*, July 14, 2011. www.gizmag.com.

28. Quoted in "Advanced Solution for Harnessing Light Winds," *UnderstandingNano.com.* www.understandingnano.com.

29. Quoted in "Rice Unveils Super-Efficient Solar-Energy Technology," *UnderstandingNano.com.* www.understandingnano.com.

30. Quoted in Mary Henderson, "Carbon Nanotechnology Lowers Cost of Hydrogen Fuel Cell," *The Better World Project*. www.betterworldproject.org.

31. Jesus de La Fuente, *Graphenea*. www.graphenea.com.
32. Quoted in Dexter Johnson, "Graphene Origami Boxes Exceed Hydrogen Storage Targets," *IEEE Spectrum,* March 13, 2014. http://spectrum.ieee.org.
33. Quoted in Elizabeth Landau, "Tiny Technologies Could Produce Big Energy Solutions," CNN. www.cnn.com.
34. Quoted in Landau, "Tiny Technologies Could Produce Big Energy Solutions."

Chapter 4: Warfare on the Nanoscale

35. Quoted in Lance Laytner, "America's Super Soldiers," *Edit International.* www.editinternational.com.
36. Quoted in "Developing 'Second Skin' Military Nanotechnology Fabric to Repel Chemical and Biological Agents," *Nanowerk*, November 27, 2012. www.nanowerk.com.
37. Quoted in Allison Barrie, "Nanofoam Could Lead to New Body Armor, UC San Diego Researchers Say," *Fox News*, April 2, 2013. www.foxnews.com.
38. Quoted in "Nanotech on the Front Lines," *Forbes*. www.forbes.com.
39. Dan Rowinski, "Connected Air: Smart Dust Is the Future of the Quantified World," *ReadWrite*, November 14, 2013. http://readwrite.com.
40. Quoted in John Gartner, "Military Reloads with Nanotech," *MIT Technology Review*, January 21, 2005. www.technologyreview.com.
41. Quoted in "Military Uses of Nanotechnology: The Future of War," *The Nano Age*. www.thenanoage.com.
42. Hitoshi Nasu, "The Future of Nanotechnology in Warfare," *Global: The Global Journal*, July 4, 2013. www.theglobaljournal.net.

Chapter 5: A World-Changing Technology

43. Quoted in Jamie Condliffe, "What Will the Future of Molecular Manufacturing Really Be Like?," *Gizmodo*. http://gizmodo.com.

44. Feynman, "There's Plenty of Room at the Bottom."
45. K. Eric Drexler, "Molecular Engineering: An Approach to the Development of General Capabilities for Molecular Manipulation," *Institute for Molecular Manufacturing*. www.imm.org.
46. Drexler, "Molecular Engineering."
47. Giulio Prisco, "Op-Ed: The Nanobots Are Coming Back," *Digital Journal*, February 11, 2015. www.digitaljournal.com.
48. Prisco, "Op-Ed: The Nanobots Are Coming Back."
49. Quoted in Katherine Bourzac, "3-D Transistors Made with Molecular Self-Assembly," *MIT Technology Review*, January 23, 2015. www.technologyreview.com.
50. Quoted in Belle Dumé, "DNA Helps Build New Materials for Controlling Light," *Nanotechweb*, April 20, 2015. http://nanotechweb.org.
51. Quoted in Condliffe, "What Will the Future of Molecular Manufacturing Really Be Like?"
52. Ralph Merkle, "Nanotechnology." www.zyvex.com.
53. Drexler, *Radical Abundance*, p. 286.

For Further Research

Books

K. Eric Drexler, *Engines of Creation: The Coming Era of Nanotechnology.* New York: Anchor Library of Science, 1986.

K. Eric Drexler, *Radical Abundance: How a Revolution in Nanotechnology Will Change Civilization.* New York: Public Affairs, 2013.

S.M. Lindsay, *Introduction to Nanoscience.* New York: Oxford University, 2010.

W. Patrick McCray, *The Visioneers: How a Group of Elite Scientists Pursued Space Colonies, Nanotechnologies, and a Limitless Future.* Princeton, NJ: Princeton University, 2012.

Ben Rogers and Jesse Adams, *Nanotechnology: Understanding Small Systems.* Boca Raton, FL: CRC, 2014.

Internet Sources

Katherine Bourzac, "3-D Transistors Made with Molecular Self-Assembly," *MIT Technology Review*, January 23, 2015. www.technologyreview.com.

Jamie Condliffe, "What Will the Future of Molecular Manufacturing Really Be Like?," *Gizmodo*, February 16, 2015. http://gizmodo.com.

Maria Doyle, "How Nanotechnology Is Gaining Momentum in Manufacturing," *Forbes*, August 25, 2014. www.forbes.com.

Belle Dumé, "DNA Helps Build New Materials for Controlling Light," *Nanotechweb*, April 20, 2015. http://nanotechweb.org.

Hitoshi Nasu, "The Future of Nanotechnology in Warfare," *Global: The Global Journal*, July 4, 2013. www.theglobaljournal.net.

Stephen Ornes, "'Smart' Clothes Generate Electricity," *Student Science*, March 23, 2015. https://student.societyforscience.org.

Websites

Center for Responsible Nanotechnology (www.crnano.org). This website examines the major societal and environmental aspects of advanced nanotechnology. It includes features and links to articles that focus on the risks and benefits of molecular manufacturing.

Foresight Institute (www.foresight.org). This website focuses on all aspects of nanotechnology as well as other transformative future technologies. It is an excellent source for articles and websites devoted to the latest advances in nanotechnology.

Nanowerk (www.nanowerk.com). This website presents a good overview of nanotechnology research and general news. It features links to blogs and other technology websites and maintains a Top 10 Spotlights list of the best current articles on nanotechnology.

National Nanotechnology Initiative (www.nano.gov). This website features information about the US government's research and development efforts in nanotechnology. It contains a comprehensive introduction to nanotech and articles about current research in the field.

Index

Picture Credits

About the Author

John Allen is a writer living in Oklahoma City.